CHARLES MOLESWORTH

GARY SNYDER'S VISION
POETRY AND THE REAL WORK

WITHDRAWN

A LITERARY FRONTIERS EDITION

UNIVERSITY OF MISSOURI PRESS

COLUMBIA, 1983

Copyright © 1983 by
The Curators of the University of Missouri
University of Missouri Press, Columbia, Missouri 65211
Library of Congress Catalog Card Number 83–6993
Printed and bound in the United States of America
All rights reserved

Library of Congress Cataloging in Publication Data

Molesworth, Charles, 1941–
  Gary Snyder's vision.

  (Literary frontiers)
  1. Snyder, Gary—Criticism and interpretation.
I. Title. II. Series.
PS3569.N88Z78   1983   811'.54   83–6993
ISBN 0–8262–0414–7

    Acknowledgment is given to New Directions Publishing Corporation
for their permission to reprint passages from the following works by
Gary Snyder: *Myths & Texts*, Copyright © 1960; *Back Country*, © 1968;
Regarding Wave, Copyright © 1970; and *Turtle Island*, Copyright © 1972.
    I wish to acknowledge with gratitude the Rockefeller Foundation
Humanities Program, with the help of whose Fellowship this work
was written.
    Also, I would like to thank Alex Silberman for many suggestions
and for reading an early draft of the book, and Michael Heller and
Jane Augustine for special assistance.

THIS BOOK IS FOR JOAN RICHARDSON
AND FOR ROBERT PICCIOTTO

CONTENTS

BOOKS BY GARY SNYDER

POETRY

Riprap and Cold Mountain Poems (1959, 1965)
Myths & Texts (1960, 1978)
The Back Country (1968)
Regarding Wave (1970)
Six Sections from *Mountains and Rivers
    without End* (1970, 1977)
Turtle Island (1974)

PROSE

Earth House Hold (1969)
The Old Ways (1977)
*He Who Hunted Birds in His Father's Village:
    Dimensions of a Haida Myth* (1979)
*The Real Work: Interviews and Talks
    1964–1978* (1980)

Three books of poetry were published in
later editions, essentially unchanged. I
have quoted from the later editions in all
cases. Much of Snyder's work that
appeared in limited editions and ephem-
era has subsequently been collected in
the books above. An English volume,
A Range of Poems (1966), contains *Riprap*
and other material.

I. Contexts

> Brecht comes and stands in an artful, crushed posture in front of the armchair in which I am sitting—he is imitating "the state"—and says, with a sidelong squint at imaginary clients: "I know, I *ought* to be abolished."
>
> —"Conversations with Brecht" by Walter Benjamin

In the nationally franchised bookstore across the boulevard from where I am writing this, there is a section marked *Philosophy*. Almost half the titles deal with Eastern cultures, mysticism, and esoterica. This may be because the clerks simply have no other place to put the writings of Ouspensky and Krishnamurti, but nevertheless it says something about the main tradition of European metaphysical thought in America during the final decades of the twentieth century. This tradition supported and developed a cognate tradition of political philosophy. In our higher branches of education it has been assumed that this political tradition, represented by such names as Hobbes, Locke, Rousseau, and Hegel, supplied at least the vocabulary, if not the answers, to our political arguments. There are myriad observations one could make about the current vitality of this body of traditional assumptions, procedures, and values. I restrict myself to two reductive possibilities. At worst, we could say that the tradition has been undermined by its followers' habits of skepticism and radical dissent, as represented in the work of Nietzsche and Marx. Furthermore, the tradition of political thought has long since been replaced by political science, and normative political visions cannot hope to withstand the allure of quantitative social policies. In turn, dissatisfaction with the rationalization and quantification of the social sciences has driven many people to brief and phantasmal refuge in arcane escapism. At best, one might argue that the genius of the tradition is its openness to a great many influences, even those of the Orient, and its affirmation of the worth of the individual, with all

1

the potentially untidy, proto-anarchic tendencies such affirmation involves. If we are to read a contemporary poet against the widest cultural context, we must at least raise these opposing views in order to sense, partly intuitively, partly critically, which aspect governs the assumptions behind the practice of lyric poetry. In this book I will try to read the work of Gary Snyder in such a context and will raise, tentatively, some related questions along the way, questions that deal with the relation of the lyric voice to historical and political vision and with the status of figurative language and mythical thought.

Snyder's work draws heavily on two sources of cultural wisdom: Buddhism and Amerindian lore. In its fundamental assumptions, his work radically dissents from the dominant values of Western society. At the same time, this dissent addresses that society, offering a countercultural matrix of social values and historical vision. In a sense Snyder's work is part of the legacy of modernism, and as such it can be seen, incorrectly in my judgment, as anticultural. The primitive strain of modernism often appears aggressively anticultural, set not only in an attitude of opposition but in one of rejection as well. However, Snyder does not propose an anarchic or totally unlimited choice among social values, using Buddhism, say, as merely an example of "otherness." Rather, he synthesizes—perhaps we should say synergizes—an amalgam of parts of various cultures into a coherent, stable vision. Unlike many other contemporary poets, Snyder has provided an explicit formulation of his vision; although this formulation does not contain all the detail and tension of the vision as it is expressed in the poetry, it is one we can begin with:

> As a poet I hold the most archaic values on earth. They go back to the upper Palaeolithic: the fertility of the soil, the magic of animals, the power-vision in solitude, the terrifying initiation and rebirth, the love and ecstasy of the dance, the common work of the tribe. (*Myths & Texts*, p. viii)

Clearly this resonates with the primitive strain in modernism, as well as with a concern for the mythical modes of thought that are a legacy of nineteenth-century compara-

2

tive mythology and anthropology. But the social consciousness involved in the last phrase, as well as the historical vision embedded in the opening sentence, reflect what will be the central focus of my examination of Snyder's works. The values associated with nature can be seen as part of Snyder's romantic heritage, and they—along with their relation to the social and historical framework—will be discussed in more detail later.

Much of Snyder's work involves the establishment of an alternative vision, especially a vision of the role of the poet. Indeed much of the weight of the work's total force hinges on just this redefinition of the poet's powers and place in a society gone dangerously off-course. We can see part of this redefinition by alternative in Snyder's description of the twin poles of Chinese poetry. In a symposium on "Chinese Poetry and the American Imagination," in *Ironwood* 17 (1981), he offered this formulation:

> In a simple way, I think, our first Anglo-American received view of the Chinese poets was that they were civil servants. And in a simplified way, there is some truth in this. There were extremes as great perhaps as Han Yu on the one side as a rigorous, benevolent, socially-minded poet, Confucianist all his life; and at the other end, perhaps a poet like Han Shan who speaks entirely from the hermit's habitat. Yet in actual fact, these two kinds of poetry which I am artificially separating for the moment, were generally produced by the same people. Now to add to the complexity, we have no real models in Occidental poetry of poets who either were staunch, quiet, solid civil-servants involved in responsible positions in society for a whole lifetime as a regular type of poet, nor do we have on the other hand a real tradition of hermit's poetry in the Occident. So it's all the more interesting to see that these two types of roles of poetry were both in China coming from the same individuals, often at different stages within one lifetime, or in some cases, it was just a matter of literally changing hats—Confucian hat to Taoist hat while on a trip to the country.

One response to this would contend that it is the achievement of the Western lyric poet to maintain an eccentric relation to the dominant social values, neither fully ac-

3

cepting nor rejecting them. The cultural commissar and the hermit are corrosive roles in this view, and they undermine what is valuable in our tradition: poets are *un*-acknowledged legislators, and this negative centrality, if you will, benefits everyone. The antinomian streak in contemporary American poetry, for example, rests on a feeling that the individual imagination, even if (or especially when) it indulges in a sort of surrealist whimsy, satisfies a human need that is importantly pre- or transsocial. Crudely put, another axiom has it that poems are for private issues, while public concerns are the province of prose fiction. Christopher Caudwell reversed this axiom in his *Illusion and Reality*, but his argument—since poetry draws on preconscious awareness it must perforce deal with shared and communal values—has not generally held sway. But Snyder obviously operates with something like this view in mind, though he realizes the Chinese "solution" is not likely to be readily adapted by American poets.

Or is it? Instead of a solution to be adapted, the poet might face a dialectic to be accepted. In the article quoted above, Snyder goes on to speak of the role of the hermit poet that attracted him, whereas a poet like Ezra Pound felt drawn to the role of the writer with "political power in a strong bureaucracy." But surely Pound was both a political poet and a troubadour singing of personal ideals, and just as surely Snyder is a poet of hermitlike isolation as well as a social visionary. In the Western tradition, and perhaps especially in some contemporary American poets, the struggle is less with either one role or the other than with the mediation between both. As with the Chinese poets, we have two kinds of poetry coming from individual poets. This possibility became especially marked in the late 1960s, with the work of such poets as Ginsberg, Bly, Levine, Rich, Levertov, and Kinnell, among others. Obviously much has been written about this period, including a great deal about the role of certain critical reading habits, fostered by the hegemony of New Critical formalism in the universities. Gradually, however, since the 1960s it has become possible to see lyric poetry as incorporating materials and concerns once considered impure or political in the pejorative sense. Nonetheless, Snyder's work still suffers from the remaining bias, and many readers find his work either tendentious politically or insufficiently complex in terms of irony, paradox, and other formalist values.

Still, Snyder is bold enough to formulate a political and historical vision, for as he goes on to say in the symposium:

> actually poetry in a healthy, stable society (in which poets are not forced willy-nilly to all be revolutionaries) does influence the behavior of lovers, and it does make one think of one's parents, and put importance on friendship, and give meaning to history and culture, and improve public manners . . . yes, poetry should do that.

At this point we almost have to raise the question of totalization. In bringing up such a question, the specter of Hegel or Kant or some systematic pre-twentieth-century philosophy also rises. Can poetry ever regain its comprehensive, panoptic sense of being a form of knowledge that lays claim to all realms of experience? If philosophy has abandoned this role, how might poetry presume to shoulder it? Have we stopped talking of a verbal artifact; stopped thinking of the short, well-made lyric; and instead shifted to a nearly mystical sense of something like cultural gracefulness or the metaphoric imagination in general? And by such standards will not Snyder's poetry be severely tested (as would anyone's)? Are we not better off without the poet posing as Victorian sage, without all the by now built-in self-deception and exaggeration such a role entails?

But Snyder's work, judged as success or failure or a mixture of both, raises questions very like these. Standing in a tradition reaching from Pound to Olson and on to Ginsberg, Snyder takes seriously that strain in modernism that equates the style and the man and thus links the aesthetics of the work with the ethics of the vision. Ordinarily this connection is understood in a reductively psychologized way, as a sort of Flaubertian fastidiousness that

5

infects the work or spills over from the writing into one's daily habits. This sort of paradigm—a version of expressive causality on a personal level where character and individual destiny become the master terms—dies hard. It is easy to dismiss Snyder as a countercultural spokesman, an ex-Beatnik turned ecologist, whose main statement is his life-style. I prefer to see him as a visionary poet, but one who operates in a context—historical, political, and literary—that no longer assumes that political vision can be derived from, or cognate with, anything like confidence in traditional metaphysical truth or the ultimate harmonizing of established theological concepts. He writes within the conditions established by the "secular historical consciousness" that Susan Sontag says governs all European culture since the French Revolution. Snyder has praised Chinese poetry for satisfying the "thirst for natural, secular clarity" and thus invigorating poets who were "tired of heroics and theologies." Even allowing for his idealization of Chinese poetry, Snyder plainly desires a poetry that matters, at the levels of mundane awareness and cosmic consciousness. He also knows that such a totalizing vision must be testable in the very details of sensory experience, a key point that I will discuss at length later.

Here I might do well to say a few things about political vision, especially about its function and scope. Snyder's vision is not intended to deal primarily with practical matters but rather with presuppositions and ultimate values. As such it clearly contains religious dimensions, though not of an ecclesiastical kind, and it seeks to understand some "ground of ultimate concern." For Snyder this ground is the harmonious interaction of man and nature ("the fertility of the soil, the magic of animals"). In turn this grounding contributes to an illumination of purpose rather than to proving or disproving the efficacy of certain actions. Though concerned with practical consequences and even with physical laws, Snyder looks toward a total process of nature to which the human species must submit. In one sense utopian, in another sense apocalyptic, this total process relies heavily on the metaphor of "interbirth," that is, the creation of a "world of ongoing recurrence-comradeship with the landscape and continual exchanges of being and form and position." Interbirth is thus like the deified Nature of the romantic tradition, but it has a fuller sense of being an empirical base that rests on a humane understanding of the scientific method. This "empirically observable interconnectedness," as Snyder calls it in *Earth House Hold*, governs and is part of a physical, lived world, but it is also apprehensible only through a properly ordered consciousness. This ordered consciousness acts as the key to the vision and as its highest expression. In his later writings Snyder stresses the "Mind" as the most beautiful of poems, and this stress opens his project to the charge of excessive idealism. But the physical dimension of the vision remains a crucial one. Vision arises from experience but does not rest there, as it attempts to transform experience into wisdom. Some critics see Thoreau as moving from a transcendentalist view of the world to one laden with facts, ending his career as little more than a passive observer of natural phenomena. Perhaps we can see Snyder as tracing the reverse of this course, moving from dense factuality to a prizing of mental operations. This simplifies too much, to be sure, especially when we remember Thoreau's injunction to honor the single fact, for we never know when it might flower into truth.

As for the scope of his vision, Snyder develops it in large measure within the traditional assumptions of romanticism. By making a version of natural process his master term, he necessarily emphasizes some concerns and diminishes others, as all visionaries do. In political terms his vision opposes the main developments of European political thought as it developed in the late eighteenth and nineteenth centuries. During this time, the tradition that came to be known as classical liberalism gradually displaced political questions with social ones.[1] Locke, Adam Smith, and others inaugurated three main themes: a lim-

1. This discussion is heavily indebted to Sheldon Wolin, *Politics and Vision* (New York: Little, Brown & Co., 1960), especially chap. 9, "Liberalism and the Decline of Political Philosophy."

ited government committed to preserving security rather than enunciating goals; the establishment of "society" as a mechanism with its own laws and processes; and the notion of control by impersonal forces, eventually to be identified with the "hidden hand" of the marketplace. Since society was seen as spontaneous and self-regulating, it was accorded the status of a natural force. Political power and authority came more and more to be seen as coercive and hence needed to be minimized. This body of thought, obviously, persists as one of the main sources of American politics today, where we are often asked to elect to high political office people who claim their most important qualification is that they are *not* politicians. But Snyder's vision largely ignores the social issues—that is, the mechanisms of daily life and such mundane concerns as urban experience and bureaucratized work schemes—in favor of the political, such as the question of our relation to the environment, the blindness engendered by loyalty to the nation-state, and our allegiance to ideological systems based on domination and waste. What Snyder calls the "power-vision in solitude" stands as a presocial or even antisocial form of cognition, but it nevertheless contains a set of implicit political values.

A word of caution is needed here. By focusing more on the political than on the social, Snyder not only opens himself to the charge of impracticality but also risks having all he says dismissed as merely metaphorical. Such notions as "interbirth," drawn from the aboriginal tribes of Australia, provide for a rhetorical and poetic integration of various forces, and even levels of awareness. This sort of notion (or governing image) springs from a desire for unity, a need to locate and name a central or centering force. The truth of the notion, then, is not measurable in strict scientific terms. But, ironically, just such a central visionary metaphor is operating in the idea of the market's "invisible hand." What was natural for Adam Smith has become what is chiefly unnatural for Snyder, as the commodification of time and labor brought about by market relations has become the main cause and support for alienation from the realm of fertility, initiation, rebirth, and so forth. Many people today scoff at the unreality of the metaphor of an invisible hand, even as they feel its very real widespread consequences in the cultural revolution of nineteenth-century entrepreneurial capitalism. The metaphor of the invisible hand played a successful role in the shift from mercantilism to free-market capitalism, just as the metaphoric vision of "social Darwinism" helped develop market capitalism into monopoly capitalism. Snyder's vision of man and nature remains unlikely to prevail unless the world's political and economic order changes fundamentally. Most people agree such change is frequently accompanied and even explicated by such visionary metaphors, but few would acknowledge that the metaphors are genuinely causative of such fundamental changes.

Eventually I hope to show how Snyder's vision not only responds to but putatively corrects the values of multinational capitalism. Furthermore, and more problematically, I will try to show that his vision is made possible by the very conditions it criticizes. There is irony here, even paradox, and not merely of an aesthetic sort. For example, Snyder's idealism acts as the highest expression of his vision, the natural outgrowth of his emphasis on awareness and mindfulness. Simultaneously, however, the idealism reflects the limitations of his vision and is intimately linked with the relative quietism and retreat from political activity that have been part of Snyder's career since 1970. While criticizing American policies that affect global issues, Snyder still operates within an indigenous American political tradition that reaches back through Thoreau to Jefferson's ideal of the husbandman.[2] The limits of this tradition generate a paradox that shapes the discourse of most dissenting visions, since the critical voice is shaped in part by values inextricably mixed with those it rejects. How we read Snyder's poetry will of course be determined by whether we see the paradox as inevitably linked

2. For Jefferson, see Leo Marx, *The Machine in the Garden: Technology and the Pastoral Idea in America* (New York: Oxford University Press, 1960), chap. 3.

with the tension necessary to any good art, or whether we use it to judge the vision negatively as a literary displacement of concerns more properly addressed by other means.

For several centuries now, the language of poetry, and its traditional status as discourse, has been taken as a form of contemplative activity, devoted to aesthetic aims and qualities. Though it is a truism to say this has not always been so, and indeed need not be so, Snyder's poetry rests uneasily on just such a truism. As Michael Oakeshott put it in his *The Voice of Poetry in the Conversation of Mankind* (1959), the "emancipation" of poetry from practical ends is a "comparatively new and still unassimilated experience." For Oakeshott, poetry always plays a frankly escapist role, though its integration back into the wholeness of our experience is to be imagined in terms of a "conversational relationship," in which different kinds of voices mingle without hierarchic ranking or the seeking of a conclusion. However, Snyder defines the function of poetry differently, as a twofold form of clarification and transmission. Here is one passage, from an interview in *The Real Work:*

> the function of poetry is not only the intensification and clarification of the implicit potentials of the language, which means a sharpening, a bringing of more delight to the normal functions of language and making maybe language even work better since communication is what it's about. But on another level poetry is intimately linked to any culture's fundamental worldview, body of lore, which is its myth-base . . . the source of much of its values . . . That foundation is most commonly expressed and transmitted in the culture by poems.

Here Snyder's debt to Pound stands out (he quotes Pound later in the interview), and some of the larger influences of post-Enlightenment poetic theory are also apparent. Poetry in this context may tend to become autotelic, since it has its own medium, language, as one of its subjects. But to the extent poetry transmits value it has practical ends, however deferred or remote. Poetry thus becomes a form of mediation, and its activities of integration, free play, and symbolmaking can serve as paradigms of possible social harmony, for which language itself is a necessary if not sufficient condition (a "bringing of more delight to the normal functions of language").

A little later in the same interview Snyder formulates the function of poetry a bit differently, and it is here that I would say another form of mediation occurs, between the social and the individual, the historical and the transcendent:

> The value and function of poetry can be said in very few words. One side of it is *in-time,* the other is *out-of-time.* The in-time side of it is to tune us in to *mother* nature and *human* nature so that we live *in time,* in our societies in a way and on a path in which all things can come to fruition equally, and together in harmony. A path of beauty. And the out-of-time function of poetry is to return us to our own true original nature at this instant forever. And those two things happen, sometimes together, sometimes not, here and there and all over the world, and always have.

Here poetry has a more operative or curative function ("a path in which all things can come to fruition") as well as an even more contemplative or aesthetic one ("our own true original nature at this instant forever"). Obviously this demands a great deal from poetry. The emphasis on "original nature" recalls the claims Heidegger made for Hölderlin's poetry; one of the poet's sayings that Heidegger glosses maintains that language has "been given to man so . . . he may affirm what he is." The other, curative function, focused as it is on the social and historical dimension of our existence, rests on an equally large claim, and, as I've suggested, one that is less available to our cultural expectations at the moment. Snyder has virtually gone outside the currently dominant literary traditions of modern European culture to make these claims, and his use of Buddhist and Amerindian material can be read as either a critique or a radical reimagining of that tradition.[3] But I would here invoke one of the critical axioms of the

3. See the discussion of Snyder in Charles Altieri, *Enlarging the Temple: New Directions in American Poetry during the 1960's* (Lewisburg, Pa.: Bucknell University Press, 1979), pp. 131–50. This is clearly the best discussion of Snyder, attentive to all the philosophical and aesthetic problems.

tradition of humanist literature: we must judge a writer, in part at least, by the criteria he or she raises in the work itself. One corollary of this axiom, by the way, is that Snyder's prose becomes an important context in which to read his poetry, but this does not mean we have to accept the prose pronouncements and simply see if the poetry enacts or embodies them. Rather we must ask about the ethical, spiritual, and political coherence and worth of the vision as it is expressed in both the poetry and the prose. Those who judge Snyder by his life-style or his role as cultural hero are at least partially right in not reading him merely or exclusively as a lyric poet. That context is both primary and insufficient.

Riprap

The dominant poetics of *Riprap* is that of the relatively extensive tradition of imagism and objectivism, whose main clarions are Pound's belief that "the natural object is always the adequate symbol" and Williams's "no ideas but in things." This concentration of sensory attention results from many causes, perhaps the chief one being a mistrust of the Victorian high style with its affective moralism. But such fervent desire for vindication and sincerity lodged in the sensory realm must have deeper roots. In artists like Conrad, Woolf, and Wyndham Lewis, despite myriad differences among them, the thrust of high modernism was an attempt to create and reassemble the sensorium in such a way as to respond to the fragmentation of social life.[4] Clearly Snyder's work has its roots in this cultural struggle, which saw the longing for a unity of consciousness rise out of a sense of fragmentation and paradoxically end

4. Fredric Jameson sees modernism as "perpetuating the increasing subjectivization of individual experience and the atomization and disintegration of the older social communities . . . [while] it also embodies a will to overcome the commodification of late nineteenth-century capitalism, and to substitute for the mouldering . . . bazaar of late Victorian life the mystique and promise of some intense and heightened, more authentic experience." *Fables of Aggression: Wyndham Lewis, the Modernist as Fascist* (Berkeley: University of California Press, 1979), p. 39. I am also indebted to Jameson's later book, *The Political Unconscious*.

by contributing to that sense, as the poetic image eventually set itself against all other mental energies, such as reverie or association. Recall Clement Greenberg's notion of "dialectical conversion," in which a style pursues its aims so purely that it results in something like its opposite. Greenberg used the example of impressionism, which sought to render the truth of the perception of the natural world so vigorously that it eventually was driven to produce an art of abstraction. Likewise, the imagists sought to reenergize the prearranged world of routinized, mundane experience with such vigor that they often ended by displaying a poetry of flat surfaces devoid of any transcendent dimension. (George Oppen, the objectivist, said, "I do believe that consciousness exists and that it is consciousness of something, and that is a fairly complete theology.") Such purity of intention diminishes, however, once the polemical moment has passed. Snyder's *Riprap* embodies an extension, without polemic force, of the objectivist poetic, and it also contains an important thematic argument, one that operates throughout much of Snyder's later work as well.

The thematic center of *Riprap* is the awareness that the need for solidity and harmony can only be gained away from city life, in the processes of natural forces and cycles. Dominating the experience of the book is the "out-of-time" awareness, combined with a sense that such awareness is momentary. Further complicating the situation is an awareness that such momentary breakthroughs—out of the rationalized urban life into nature, or out of nature into a timeless order—are hard to integrate into ordinary consciousness. Also, with the objectivist poetic in mind, we should remember that all thematic statements are distortions of the spirit of *Riprap*, since that spirit is governed by the metaphor of the title. "Solidity of bark, leaf, or wall / riprap of things," as the closing poem puts it, turning the logger's riprap, "a cobble of stone laid on steep slick rock to make a trail for horses in the mountain," into a poetic of density, tight craftsmanship, and avoidance of all superfluity of word or feeling. But these lines might serve as emblem for the central concerns of the poetry:

                          A million
        Summers, night air still and the rocks
        Warm. Sky over endless mountains.
        All the junk that goes with being human
        Drops away, hard rock wavers
        Even the heavy present seems to fail
        This bubble of a heart.
        Words and books
        Like a small creek off a high ledge
    ,   Gone in the dry air.

                                        ("Piute Creek")

Not only do the products of civilization dematerialize under the aegis of a harmoniously intensified nature, but the
observer himself is borne to the edge of nonexistence. As
with the sublime of the romantic tradition, nature here
rearranges the composed consciousness at the same time
it heightens it, and an almost gnostic sense of catastrophe
makes nature look like a destructive power. This dialectic
is alluded to in the subsequent lines of this poem: "A clear,
attentive mind / Has no meaning but that / Which sees is
truly seen." The visual usurps all other forms of consciousness or intellection, although—and this is crucial—
the reciprocity of keen seeing is redemptive, or at least
stabilizing. The poem ends with these lines:

                          A flick
        In the moonlight
        Slips into Juniper shadow:
        Back there unseen
        Cold proud eyes
        Of Cougar or Coyote
        Watch me rise and go.

Clearly this is a sacramentalized nature, the more-than-
physical dimension serving to vindicate or even bless the
watchful acolyte. But the acolyte cannot name that dimension, except in the usual sort of pathetic fallacy ("proud
eyes") or by pointing past the physical ("Back there un-
seen"). So, as in much romantic nature poetry, the physical world is brought before us, or almost before us, and
the intensity of apperception, the mechanics of perceptual
events raised to a higher consciousness, serves to put us

14

into the scene and at the same time put the scene just beyond us. The things of the poem, like the stones of the riprap, are symbols of an immanent force, the awareness that stays inside its own field, and a pathway to a higher state beyond.

This liminal consciousness, this in-between awareness, becomes Snyder's thematic approach to the social order in *Riprap*. Though the majority of the poems in the book deal with natural subjects, largely or exclusively, the social order is present from the first poem and in some cases becomes the focus if not the locale of other lyrics. In "The Late Snow & Lumber Strike of the Summer of Fifty-Four," for example, with the "whole Northwest on strike," Snyder presents himself as a drifter unable to find work and unable to remain in a natural setting:

> I must turn and go back:
>   Caught on a snow peak
>   between heaven and earth
> And stand in lines in Seattle.
> Looking for work.

The world of wage-labor not only lacks the pleasures of the mountains but also creates a set of necessities and disruptions that not even the fraternity of other workers can overcome. In a later poem, "T-2 Tanker Blues," the wage-labor is not logging but working as a seaman on an oil tanker. Here, too, the awareness is largely alienated:

> Mind swarming with pictures, cheap magazines, drunk
>   brawls, low books and days at sea; hatred of
>   machinery and money & whoring my hands and
>   back to move this military oil—

Even the proselike format here indicates an unsettled mind, and the poem's images are less heightened by isolation than intensified by a jumble, a swarm. The poem breaks up into a series of counterposing claims and desires: "I will not cry Inhuman & think that makes us small and nature great." His attempts to accept the social and economic structure for what it is break down, however, and Snyder has to adopt a stellar prespective to come to terms with confusion and anger: "man, inhuman man, / at whom I look for a thousand light years from a seat / near Scorpius." The poem ends with an aestheticized version of the very instrument of the seamen's oppression: "welded plates of perfect steel." I read this poem as in many ways crucial for Snyder, because it shows how he must decide in what realm to place the socioeconomic order. In obvious ways it is an unnatural order. Yet if it is man-made it must also be the product of natural forces; the only alternative to this is to declare man, in whole or in part, unnatural or even inhuman. But the harmony of perfect seeing that Snyder has experienced in "Piute Creek" demonstrates how man does (or at least might) participate in the order of nature.

The social order, then, exists in *Riprap* almost like an absent cause. Domination by oppressive wage-labor intensifies, but does not permit full adoption of, moments of natural ecstasy. More important, such labor can be rejected only on grounds that deny humanity to man and separate him irremediably from the natural order. One way out of this tension is to seek another culture, one where the moments of ecstasy have more social authority, as it were, where men respect the intensity of the transitory and the nobility of the ordinary scale of needs and appetites—things that the entrepreneurial capitalism of logging and oil tankers does not tolerate. This other culture is Japan. There are only four poems in *Riprap* set in Japan, and only the subsequent shape of Synder's interests makes their importance clear. These four poems all contain social groupings, and three of the four deal with family relations, an aspect of the social order virtually absent from the poems set in the Pacific Northwest and on tankers. In *Regarding Wave,* as we will see, the importance of family relations and the locale of Japan coalesce, as Snyder's marriage to Masa, a Japanese woman, serves as the center of that later book.

As a group, these early poems about Japan show us Snyder as an outsider, but one who observes carefully and with interest and who more often than not is content to praise an agricultural society, or, where the Japanese live in cities, to see them as still retaining the family ties of a pre-urban way of life. In the longest of the poems, he calls Japan "a great stone garden in the sea." An almost Whitman-like embrace develops in this pastoral setting, and the feelings of the poet modulate into an acceptance of death and impermanence and finally into something like a Buddhist resolution of all consciousness in the void.

> Seeing in open doors and screens
> The thousand postures of all human fond
> Touches and gestures, glidings, nude,
> The oldest and nakedest women more the sweet,
> And saw there first old withered breasts
> Without an inward wail of sorrow and dismay
> Because impermanence and destructiveness of time
> In truth means only, lovely women age—
> But with the noble glance of I Am Loved
> From children and from crones, time is destroyed.
> The cities rise and fall and rise again
> From storm and quake and fire and bomb,
> The glittering smelly ricefields bloom,
> And all that growing up and burning down
> Hangs in the void a little knot of sound.
>
> ("A Stone Garden")

This passage works with a plain-style stateliness that mixes a small portion of guilt (the "bomb" of the twelfth line) and a larger part of innocence ("saw there first") and resolves into an image that is partly liminal and partly a condensed emblem of the poem's antithetical, yet complementary, gestures of awareness. The overall sense strikes me as somewhat utopian, yet fully immanent at the same time; in this the structure of the passage resembles the resolution of "Piute Creek" and several of the other poems of nature in the book. Japan, then, embodies the most positive aspects of Snyder's political vision in these early works. He must pastoralize it as a setting, and he must exist in it as a relatively rootless wanderer. Yet just like the nature he sees either as a logger or as a forest ranger, the place serves as a location of real work, and his very rootlessness is what enables him to see conditions the indigenous population cannot bring to heightened consciousness. Snyder's political sense originates in his experience of the wilderness but becomes articulated only in a civilized setting that comes to him with the freshness and integrity of a new land, "a stone garden in the sea." The place itself becomes liminal, partaking of the jewel-like and the earthy: "glittering smelly ricefields." Liminality becomes a token for the "growing up and burning down" of time's own force, and so the ideal society is both in and out of time.

This combination of an immanent view with a utopian one crystallizes in the ending of "A Stone Garden." The exact force of the closing remains ambiguous, in part because the poet speaks as a husband, but the role seems more of a mythical than an actual one. "This marriage never dies," he says, apparently speaking of the human and social needs that the family addresses universally as well as personally. Then Snyder returns to the theme of the dialectic of growth and destruction.

> Delight
> Crushes it down and builds it all again
> With flesh and wood and stone,
> The woman there—she is not old or young.
>
> Allowing such distinctions to the mind:
> A formal garden made by fire and time.

One is reminded faintly of Auden's characterization of "sad Eros, builder of cities, / And weeping anarchic Aphrodite." But with Snyder the two great forces of destruction and growth—fire and time—create a garden state rather than an urban center. Also, the last two lines can be read at another level, taking the entire last line as in apposition to "mind." If mind is a formal garden, it operates as such because it contains the orders of nature and human experience, counterbalancing in formalized symmetry the powers of refinement, conflagration, growth, and decay.

In this earliest of his books, Snyder's preoccupation with mental structures appears as an important concern, set against the kind of relatively unstructured cognition provided by the meditation on natural processes. But mind will serve, of course, as the great mediator of both

18

the social and the natural order, as it does increasingly in Snyder's later books. What I have called liminality, or threshold consciousness, acts as one of the chief powers of mind for Snyder. Though such consciousness can be subsumed under the heading of irony, since it deals with a doubleness or suspension between two orders of meaningfulness or value, it more properly belongs to the poetic of field composition made most explicit by Charles Olson in "Projective Verse." If we look at the end of the title poem of *Riprap*, we can see that Snyder does not offer his dense images as only blocks or stones, thrown into the poem with a longed-for palpability in order to combat sensory drift or imprecision. Rather, the density of words and things contains a kind of impacted or solidified energy as well as a merely material dimension. This energized aspect of the "cobble" of rocklike words defines the mind's power to move from one solid place to another, both creating and exploring a field of awareness for itself. Snyder introduces another, ancillary comparison to clarify the mountaineer's "riprap"—one of "worlds like an endless / four-dimensional / Game of *Go*." This is a Japanese game much like the American child's hopscotch, where a rock or heavy object is thrown to determine the possibility and order of movement. The game utilizes a combination of will and accident, and it tests the limits of both by bringing them into play with one another. Likewise with the mind, or at least the mind as it is structured and reflected in and through the poem, for the mind creates a field of forces, rather than striving for a fixed object or floundering in unobjectified process. Here is how "Riprap" ends:

> In the thin loam, each rock a word
>   a creek-washed stone
> Granite: ingrained
>   with torment of fire and weight
> Crystal and sediment linked hot
>   All change, in thoughts,
> As well as things.

The mental world and the object world are places of constant change, where an apparently granitic solidity conceals a process of flux and even "torment." So the objectivism of Snyder should never be understood as a lapidary poetic, or a static building of mosaic patterns, but rather as a "trail" of cobbled stones that leads to a higher state. Yet the higher state is impossible to reach without the very dense and lithic underpinning of close observation. "No visionary without the visual" might be a way of summarizing it.

The habits of mind that Snyder exhibits in dealing with the natural world, and the grammar of understanding that these habits generate and are supported by, are, as I've suggested, analogous to those he uses for the social world. His utopia remains a place of social bonds and values that work in an immanent way, unsanctioned by any larger theological order. What provides the transtemporal identity of the social unit is, paradoxically, time itself, but time understood· as an order we are in and out of simultaneously. Again, to return briefly to "T-2 Tanker Blues," the awareness of the human order has to be drawn up from a remote stellar vantage point as well as from a very proximate shipboard perspective:

> And there is
> nothing vaster, more beautiful, remote, unthink-
>   ing (eternal rose-red sunrise on the surf-great
>   rectitude of rocks) than man, inhuman man,
> At whom I look for a thousand light years from a seat
>   near Scorpius, amazed and touched by his con-
>   cern and pity for my plight, a simple star,
> Then trading shapes again. My wife is gone, my girl
>   is gone, my books are loaned, my clothes are
>   worn, I gave away a car; and all that happened
>   years ago. Mind & matter, love & space are
>   frail as foam on beer. Wallowing on and on,
> Fire spins the driveshaft of this ship.

We can see that the threat of insubstantiality haunts Snyder not only when he faces the immensity of nature but also when he considers the object-world of the social order. Here the solidity of riprap meets its negative counterpart in the frail foam of beer, as "man, inhuman man" becomes the focus, in place of the "million summers" and "endless mountains" of "Piute Creek."

To separate, somewhat cruelly and crudely, the twin poles of Snyder's dialectic—in time and out of time, fire as energy and destruction, man as beautiful and as inhuman—deprives the work of some of its power. That power must, ultimately, be a rhetorical one, contained and assembled through the shapes and urgings of the poems. But to see the grounds of that power we have to understand not only its workings but also its materials. The social realm in *Riprap* seems to provide considerably less material than the world of nature, though Snyder sees the workings of both in similar ways. Political vision in *Riprap* acts more as a form of meditation than as one of transformation, and it is not altogether unfair to say that Snyder uses a very idealized, pastoral view of Japan to address problems in America that he otherwise cannot resolve. Whether the view he does provide can function as a practical resolution in American terms is a question that Snyder at the early point of his career was unwilling or even unable to formulate. The second edition of *Riprap* contained Snyder's translations of the "Cold Mountain Poems" of Han-shan, a hermit-poet of the T'ang dynasty. Obviously these poems are part of Snyder's reaction to the politics of America in the late 1950s—a hermit's isolation and gadfly criticism seemed a very likely response to the Cold War ideology and social conservatism of the immediate postwar era. The last of Han-shan's twenty-four brief poems goes like this:

When men see Han-shan
They all say he's crazy
And not much to look at—
Dressed in rags and hides.
They don't get what I say
& I don't talk their language.
All I can say to those I meet:
"Try and make it to Cold Mountain."

The role of the hermit presents a reconfiguration of the role of prophet (or vice versa, of course, though which role is the ground and which the figure remains a very moot question), and Snyder is clearly attracted to both. To put it reductively for the moment, Snyder's vision depends in part on his rhetorical ground: near Scorpius a thousand light-years away, on Cold Mountain as a hermit, on a tanker as a wage-laborer, or in the Sierra Nevadas as a woodsman and acolyte of nature.

With a phrase like "I don't talk their language," a myriad of political problems can be confronted and apparently resolved. The phrase is, of course, a refusal to locate oneself in the others' context, and it can be a criticism of that context as well. The last lines of Han-shan's poem implicitly judge the others' context as inferior to the poet's. This gesture lies near the heart of Snyder's project, but it does not fully determine the outcome. What we will see in the following discussion is that Snyder gradually sharpens his political view and thus gradually develops his visionary metaphors, or master terms. This development and these terms result in part from the number of trips Snyder took between Japan and America in the twenty years or so after the poems of *Riprap*. The bicultural or transcultural vocabulary and grammar shaped by such travel allowed Snyder the liminal perspective he needed on political ideas, and his freedom from a blind commitment to the nation-state is both the cause and the result of such a perspective. Ironically, however, Snyder's political vision puts a great premium on rootedness and respect for, and knowledge of, one's immediate and regional environment. Again, what is the ground and what is the figure? Should we see Snyder's impulses to play the role of hermit as the only answer to a politically repugnant and intractable situation? Or is his eventual adoption of the role of prophet a clear response to the need to look beyond the immediate situation? The retreat to the mountain and the call for an order beyond the present limits of space and time: these are traditional gestures for both the European and the Oriental political vision. But for Snyder the answering gesture might be described as a belief that there is "no political vision without a personal revitalization."

Though *Riprap* and *Myths & Texts* were written more or
less simultaneously, in the mid 1950s, the books differ no-
ticeably.[5] *Myths & Texts* feels more complex, as if the somewhat restrictive aesthetic of objectivism had broadened to
include a wider social horizon and a deeper mythical
grounding. *Myths & Texts* also demonstrates Snyder's
ability to structure a book as a complex whole. As I will
argue in more detail shortly, the book presents in its three
sections a range of differing temporal senses. Furthermore, the title reflects a dual awareness that runs throughout the book, one that Snyder consciously borrowed from
the methodology of ethnographic studies. The textual
realm is the sensory world, the world of experience and
daily activities, whereas the mythic realm contains the
imaginative and mental constructs that generate and preserve spiritual and cultural values. Snyder's honors thesis, written at Reed College in 1951 and published as *He
Who Hunted Birds in His Father's Village: The Dimensions of a
Haida Myth,* clearly shows he had mastered such a methodology in academic terms. What *Myths & Texts* makes
clear is how such skill could serve as the basis for a deep-
ening of his poetic ability. But while Snyder's thesis took
one myth and studied it in the context of all available
information on the tribe who "authored" it, Snyder's second book used the cross-fertilization of many myths from
many cultures to illumine a single set of concerns. Speaking very broadly, I would say *Myths & Texts* attempts to
clarify the problem that *Riprap* portrayed but did not resolve, namely how to integrate the heightened conscious-

5. A point made by others, notably Robert Kern, "Clearing the
Ground: Gary Snyder and the Modernist Imperative," *Criticism* 19, 2
(Spring 1977): 158–77. Kern, however, also argues that the Japan poems
in *Riprap* are "lightweight" and "off the track for Snyder." I would see this
opinion as the result of reading Snyder too narrowly in autotelic or phenomenological contexts. This can often happen despite (or as a result of?)
reading him as "radical" in aesthetic terms.

ness that the study of nature produces into a coherent social existence. To do this, Snyder had to reimagine the political order, a task that essentially occupied him throughout his next four books of poetry and three prose volumes.

Part of the process of reimagining the polis necessarily involves developing a view of history. This, in turn, involves the three senses of temporality that are explored in *Myths & Texts*. But before looking in detail at this book, I would like to offer, by way of contrast, a view of history as it has been developed by one of Snyder's contemporaries, Adrienne Rich. To anticipate, Rich largely centers her historical vision on the individual, whereas Snyder's vision deals more with a nearly anonymous group of historical subjects. This crucial distinction works as both cause and effect in relation to the two poets' historical values and master-terms and no doubt owes something to the differences in temperament and experience between the two. To objectify these differences, however, I will borrow some terms from Nietzsche's essay "On the Use and Abuse of History." These terms will distinguish between and among some of the modes of history that are available to anyone who tries to think historically, especially if such historical thinking is done in order to serve social and political goals. In this essay Nietzsche defines three types of historical writing, though the first, antiquarianism, does not concern us here. Instead, we can look at the other two types, namely monumental and critical history.

Monumental history sees historical events as exemplifying patterns and forces through great individuals. It condemns the pettiness of the present and helps battle for a better future. But it is flawed because it romanticizes the past and undermines the present by leading people to think all the great deeds have already been accomplished. The second form, critical history, seeks to place all of the past before the bar of judgment; it can overturn present pieties based on received ideas. But, again, it has a flaw, for carried too far it generates an excess of ironic consciousness, and it ends by believing that the past *should* be destroyed. What is needed is a mixture of modes and an awareness that it is always dangerous, as Nietzsche argued, to attempt to create a past "*a posteriori* from which we might spring, against that from which we do spring." Yet mankind is burdened with memory, and so we have a history whether we will it or not. Nietzsche's ideal historian would be an interested artist who integrates things, identifying unity and imposing it where it is absent. With this high ideal before us, and with an awareness of Nietzsche's conflation of the historical and the aesthetic as our passkey, let us look at the two poets.

For Adrienne Rich the insertion of the self into history takes on a configuration marked by torsions and imponderables. Her lesbian/feminist ideology has led her to identify clear patterns of victimization and guilt, and her valuing of matriarchal virtues over those she defines as patriarchal is unequivocal.[6] With such force of vision dominating the direction of Rich's growth and concerns, a reader might wonder whether the lyric values of ironic tension or self-dramatization have any part in Rich's poetry. But while these values are less important to Rich than some others—such as belief in process and the self-reflexive questioning of language—they are still a part of this poet's central concerns. I would argue, in fact, that it is irony brought to a paradoxical pitch and the problem of self-representation that dominate Rich's poetic struggles and that these struggles are both clarified and exacerbated by her confrontation with her historical vision.

There are two parts to Rich's struggle, and they can be stated as two paradoxes. First, how can women create a matriarchal society without seizing power and male-dominated institutions, since such seizure would itself be a

6. Rich defines patriarchy as "any kind of group organization in which males hold dominant power and determine what parts females shall and shall not play. . . . At the core of patriarchy is the individual unit with its division of roles, its values of private ownership, monogamous marriage, emotional possessiveness, the 'illegitimacy' of a child born outside legal marriage, the unpaid domestic services of the wife, obedience to authority, judgement, and punishment for disobedience." From *On Lies, Secrets and Silence: Selected Prose, 1966–1978* (New York: Norton & Co., 1979), pp. 78–79. The problem for Rich is whether or not *any* social forms are possible without authority and the structures in which it is embodied.

patriarchal act? Second, how can the fully individuated life-historical individual make cause with, and speak for, the majority of humanity—that is, the many nameless and faceless women who are the victims of male oppression— and yet retain her individuality? Both of these questions are versions of the two main crises in all revolutionary thought and action, but Rich would almost certainly reject such an identification as a male ruse designed either to distance or to defuse the struggle women are pursuing. I will not, therefore, explore these paradoxes under the rubric of revolutionary thought in general; rather I will concentrate on how they animate Rich's poetry, specifically her most recent book, *A Wild Patience Has Taken Me This Far.*

In "Images," the opening poem of this book, Rich agonizes over an issue that has served to focus her work over the previous two decades, namely the dream of a language of total presence. This opening poem puts the matter rather fiercely, in fact, since what it envisions is a state where the poet can "become / free of speech at last." The ambiguity of this formulation—whether she means she can speak completely openly, or that she need not speak at all—is rather plainly tilted toward the second possibility. The speaker and her female lover lie in bed, trapped in a city that contains all the violence, destruction, and oppression of patriarchal society. The urban landscape, with its "updraft / of burning life" and its "tongueless cries," is dominated by men who are "lynching" women in the name of "freedom of speech." In contrast to this scene of horror, the poet offers a place where she was "innocent of grammar," "washed clean / of the guilt of words." This place—unnamed and largely unspecified, though it is among "time-battered stones" and "near the sea"—seems to produce a mythic feminine figure:

> she of the several faces
> staring indrawn in judgment laughing for joy
> her serpents twisting her arms raised
> her breasts gazing.

Rich wants to "cry loose" her soul into that of the mythic figure and so become "free of speech at last." In the presence of this figure, however, Rich is still unable to conquer the degrading images of women produced by the male city. The poem ends in a protective, self-enclosing posture, knowing "This is the war of the images," a struggle for dominant social and sexual myths, a struggle that sets women's newly reawakened self-regard against the nightmare of patriarchal history. As we will see, Snyder shares with Rich this involvement in a war of images, a struggle to control the dominant myths of the political order.

This poem is virtually a synopsis of Rich's main themes and a paradigm of her developing self-identification since the early 1960s. In *A Wild Patience* the phrase "the dream of a common language," which was the title of her previous book of poems, is equated with another equally distant but demanding dream: the "solitude of self." These two phrases occur in one of the book's longer poems, "Culture and Anarchy," in which Rich reveals what is essentially a monumental vision of history, that is, a desire to use the figures of the past as exemplars to delineate the essential patterns and developments in history.

"Culture and Anarchy" is a poem of process in which Rich's domestic situation is sketched against a background of quotations from famous women of the past, most notably nineteenth-century feminist leaders. The title of a collection of feminist writings, *History of Woman Suffrage,* is misread as *History of Human Suffering,* and one of the main themes of the poem is the threatened status of the records of women's movements in the face of male indifference and hostility. The poem ends with an image of a vegetable, a beet, being sliced open to reveal:

> bloodlight filaments, distinct rose-purple
> striations like the oldest
> strata of a Southwestern canyon
> an undiscovered planet laid open in the lens

The lens is historical work, the restoration of the forgotten and obscured lives of women who struggled for *"emancipation / from all the crippling influences of fear,"* as the phrase of the feminist leader Elizabeth Cady Stanton expresses it. This passage goes on to say that the "strongest reason" for any woman to undertake such emancipation is the "solitude and personal / responsibility / of her own individual life." Such justification obviously explains the personal, domestic dimension of the poem, as Rich celebrates her own labor, and that of the woman with whom she lives, in rewriting the history of these heroic women. The personal dimension and the historical drama are in rare and supporting interrelationship. For the moment at least, the ideology of self-fulfillment, which the nineteenth-century feminists adapted from Protestant Christian ethics, is an effective support for twentieth-century feminist work. In other poems, however, the feeling of historical *dis*continuity will assert itself.

The poem for Ethel Rosenberg and the one entitled "Heroines" are depictions of historically significant people who have been less successful in mediating between the dimensions of personal identity and historical movements. For me the Rosenberg poem is one of the least satisfactory in the book. The initial connection rests on the chronological conjunction of the Rosenbergs' execution and Rich's own marriage. Ethel Rosenberg "becomes the extremest victim," but her politics are finally unknown to anyone; she is seen as a "family monster," and her relatives testify against her. As for Rich herself, the poet presents very little detail of her own development except to call her marriage a "separate death." Yet Rich thrusts herself and her own sensibility into the center stage of the poem, much as Yeats does at the beginning of "Easter Sunday, 1916," a poem I personally find flawed by such a rhetorical strategy, though I see where others locate its greatness as a lyric poem in just this gesture. The weakest point of Rich's poem, and an example of the inappropriate uses of monumental history, comes when the speaker asks Ethel Rosenberg if she would have joined in anti-pornography marches. Needless to say, no sure answer is offered, though the very tone of the question implies a criticism of the older woman by the younger. Eventually Rich is driven to ask, "Why all this exercise of hindsight?" She answers by averring that she must "allow" Ethel Rosenberg to be "at last / political in her ways not in mine / her urgencies perhaps impervious to mine." But then she ends the poem with an alternative image, that of the communist "bored with . . . 'politics'" and living alone, privatized into a female diarist existing in a room of her own: "maybe filli: g a notebook herself / with secrets she has never sold." The emotions of the poem form a mélange of pity and self-pity, something like praise and something like condescension. To put it (perhaps) too bluntly, Rich is unable to comprehend Ethel Rosenberg's historical meaning, so the tactic of using a monumental approach leaves the poem without sufficient existential resonance. Neither Rich nor the subject is convincingly drawn, in lyric or historical terms. It is almost as if the nagging question in Rich's mind, the question that originated the poem but is not resolved by it, is how can a woman of such clear historical dimensions as Ethel Rosenberg *not* be instructive in some way to late twentieth-century feminism? One can say that Rich has not found the common language between Ethel Rosenberg and herself; but in such a case is the poet to remain silent, to force the other to speak her language, or to settle for recording the very struggle that is required of all those who would seek common cause in correcting society and history's grievances?

In her essay on Emily Dickinson, Rich argues that "genius knows itself"; she goes on to speak of poetic language as a "concretization of the poetry of the world at large, the self, and the forces within the self." This formulation has three elements, and the last two elements are concerned with the self rather than the world. In reading Rich's poetry from the last twenty years, I have always felt the pressure of that self more than the weight of the poet's experiential world. This may be saying no more than that Rich is irreducibly a lyric poet, despite her extensive and intensive dealings with history and social issues. But I offer it as an explanation of another claim that I will make, namely that Rich's vision is at its root more a personal mythic construct than a social program or vision. The largest resolution of both her central paradoxes will be found in this mythic and individual vision, furthermore, and at *its* center is the figure of the mythic woman. This figure resolves one paradox by containing the unforgotten victimage of women while achieving ultimate domination, and it resolves the other by being most distinctive as a singular woman and yet a figure of multiple selves, "she of the several faces," as Rich called her in "Images."

In "Turning the Wheel," Rich again resolves a poem of process with a large historical image juxtaposed to a personal and domestic one. This poem, a sequence of eight parts, begins with a very negative picture of modern urban life, which is contrasted to the primitive tribal culture of Southwestern America. Opening with the line "No room for nostalgia here," the poem shows us a stale secular civilization built on a "poor, conquered, bulldozed desert / overridden like a hold-out / enemy village." "False history gets made all day, any day," the poem charges, and the poet seeks to right this injustice, if not by immediately altering the society at least by offering a different form of history. Rich works backward, through her own visit to the Desert Museum, through an imagined letter from Mary Jane Colter, a remarkable architect who designed many buildings for the Santa Fe Railroad, and through the culture of the Hohokam, a tribe who preceded the Hopi and Navaho and who are known as "those who have ceased." This fascination with the preterit, the "passed over," is a strategy for the future, regulating the return of the repressed and thus becoming not only a critique of present social values but also the groundwork for a future society free of patriarchal domination. (The Hohokam will also be the focus for one of the key poems in Snyder's *The Back Country*.) The last section of the sequence begins with a chthonic image, "the female core / of a continent," as the poem drifts into a dream landscape.

The dream reveals Rich's farthest-reaching image of victory and resolution, an image that restates the central figure of the book's opening poem, an image of a mythic female. Here the figure is both female and impersonal, singular and universal, destructive and "stained":

> I am travelling to the edge to meet the face
> of annihilating and impersonal time

30

> stained in the colors of a woman's genitals
> outlasting every transient violation
> a face that is strangely intimate to me.

This strange intimacy results from the fact that this is Rich's deepest, most sustaining image, one that her poetry has been moving with and toward throughout her previous four or five volumes. Its strangeness comes from its literal otherworldliness, for it is not a perceived, concrete image but rather a culmination of the war of images, the final arbiter and the final goal of history. It is Rich's gravest and most monumental image.

The poem, however, does not end with this image. Instead it has a seven-line stanza that brings the poet back to the experiential world of the actual desert, only to conclude with a personal reminiscence and an evocation of an unnamed person who is "far away," but to whom Rich can say, "I talk to you all day whatever day." For the moment, personal communication overshadows the large apocalyptic image of Mother Earth as Historical Justice. The self edges out history, in the sense that its hungers are finally more present than the forces of history, whether seen as domination or as vengeance. The "wild patience" of the book's title unites the anger and the tenderness Rich has spoken of needing in her life and work. And in her views of history and her self-dramatizations, the wildness of memorializing centuries of oppression is finally outweighed by the patience of her own individual hungers.

*　　*　　*

When we consider the poetry of Gary Snyder in the context of its possible historical vision, we see immediate comparisons with the work of Adrienne Rich. Snyder views modern civilization as at heart destructive, especially as it is manifested in mass urbanized society. The villain for Snyder is not patriarchy as such, though his poetry and essays have spoken of the need to respect and restore the feminine and even to find alternatives to the traditional nuclear family structure. But for Snyder the underlying destructive forces are what Jules Henry in *Cul-*

ture Against Man (1963) called "technological drivenness" and its complement "dynamic obsolescence." But even these social values have a more pervasive and mythological cause in Snyder's view, namely the rejection by man of his interrelatedness with nature and the natural environment. By failing to honor the immanent order and energy structure of his immediate natural surroundings, man is driven to excessive uses of energy and raw material. From this misuse springs modern society, but also the massive set of cultural expectations that accompany and support such unnatural misappropriation. Snyder has also formulated a way out of—or at least beyond—this mind-set, and his vision is somewhat more specific than that of Rich's matriarchal utopia. But, as we shall see, the solution has virtually overwhelming problems of persuasiveness, implementation, and consistency. Many of these problems are in fact rooted in, and explicable through, Snyder's view of history.

Snyder's view of history is largely one I would call critical, using the term in Nietzsche's sense. But as with Rich, Snyder's work moves constantly toward a set of mythological images. Snyder, however, balances (or gives ballast to) his mythical reasoning with an array of facts. He wants always to utilize certain scientific notions to go beyond the technological uses to which science has largely been applied in the industrialized world. In a sense, Snyder inverts the positivist scheme of history and sees the mythical-theological-scientific triad of developmental epochs as moving in an essentially negative or devolutionary pattern. He is not, however, an unreconstructed Luddite, though at times his historical vision can be quite bleak. His major image, especially in the later poetry, is a large mediation based on the powers of the mind: "Now, we are both in, and outside, the world at once. The only place this can be is the *Mind*. Ah, what a poem. It is what is, completely, in the past, present and future simultaneously, seeing being, and being seen" (*Turtle Island*, p. 114). Because Snyder envisions a solution to the ills of modern life only through a sort of Buddhist negation of the will, combined with a carefully thought-out, regionally focused consciousness of natural balances, he must rely on the grace and aesthetic power of mental states and faculties. But since he is aware that the power of the mind—in cultural, social, and political institutions and dominant values—has been as thoroughly polluted as the environment, Snyder is less than clear about how such a saving mediation might actually be effected.

One way to cure the mind is through "the power-vision in solitude," as Snyder calls it, by which he means a sort of shamanistic experience that has its roots in upper Paleolithic culture. This power-vision, and the experience that provides it, is perhaps best seen as what I have called a liminal awareness, a consciousness heightened, fed, and structured when the subject exists in between the orders of common experience. This in-betweenness is also a matter of temporal suspension and is exemplified in initiation and rebirth rituals of the sort discussed by Van Gennep and applied to literary understanding by Geoffrey Hartman. The difficulty with such experience and consciousness, as pointed out in the discussion of *Riprap*, is that they are not easily integrated back into the social order. This leads to what might be described as the quietistic side of Snyder's program, which leads him to the sort of isolated communal existence he has been involved in through the 1970s. His vision entails a tribal structure for its implementation, but as Morgan and then Engels argued in their speculations on early societal forms, the tribal principle seems inevitably to yield to a more authoritarian system of government. As the basis for society shifts from personal relations to property relations, the "state" and its functions and apparatus become necessary; Snyder offers no clear sense of how mass man can operate without property relations, even if the world's population is cut in half, as he suggests it should be. But neither Rich nor Snyder should be totally faulted for failing to provide—or even echo—a plan for achieving their post-historical visions; as poets with political visions their role is to try to unite "at a single stroke the reality of acts and the ideality of ends," as Barthes says in *Writing Degree Zero*.

What we can see as sympathetic readers is not Snyder's failure at the practical level but rather his relative fullness at the level of imaginative renderings of desire, as that imagination is embodied in Snyder's second book, *Myths & Texts*. Perhaps I should say "orders of time" rather than histories, for I will suggest that while the whole book can be read as a version of critical history, the three sections of *Myths & Texts*—"Logging," "Hunting," and "Burning"— rest on three distinct senses of the temporal order. These are, respectively, chronological or commodified time, pastoral time, and mythical time. Very roughly, these coincide with the three Greek terms for time, *chronos*, *kairos*, and *aeon*. The analogies I am suggesting are not ones Snyder planned consciously, nor is their separation into categories absolute. (For one obvious example, what I mean by commodified time cannot be encompassed by the Greek term *chronos*.) But the rough analogical relationship is one that Snyder maintains throughout his poetry, and it is one way his historical view is mediated and his vision at least putatively reintegrated into something like a praxis of daily life.

The first section, "Logging," based on Snyder's life experience, incorporates not only details and incidents from the lumber camps of the Pacific Northwest where the poet worked but also some of the early interest in Eastern culture and philosophy that he had developed in the 1950s. Here is one brief passage where these two areas are juxtaposed, from the last poem in the section:

> Shiva at the end of the kalpa:
> Rock fat, hill flesh, gone in a whiff.
> Men who hire men to cut groves
> Kill snakes, build cities, pave fields,
> Believe in god, but can't
> Believe their own senses
> Let alone Gautama. Let them die.

The Hindu deity comes at the end of a unit of cosmic time to destroy the work of those who exploit nature (and their fellowmen) because such work is self-alienating, breaking the harmony of natural and bodily wholeness. The defeatism of the last phrase, though put into the deity's mouth, is always a threat in Snyder, and as Nietzsche said, it is a pessimism that often threatens to undermine any critical history. The wage-labor of entrepreneurial capitalism must be utterly rejected rather than reformed or replaced. The phrase "Soldiers of Discontent" is used in this section to describe the workers—loggers and others—who have to survive at the bottom of the economic ladder, men who get "shot and beat up / For wanting a good bed, good pay, decent food, in the woods." But as Snyder says laconically of the phrase, "No one knew what it meant." Those caught in the system of wage-labor, forced to sell their time as a commodity, are unable to envision a different temporal order, except in nostalgic flashback and futile rebellion.

By and large, the dominant tone of this first section is guilt, a sense that the logging is bad not only because it fuels the "technological drivenness" but also because trees have long been used in myths, rituals, and sacred lore as symbols of the earth's procreative forces.

> Cybele's tree this, sacred in groves
> Pine of Seami, cedar of Haida
> Cut down by the prophets of Israel
>   the fairies of Athens
>   the thugs of Rome
>   both ancient and modern;
> Cut down to make room for the suburbs
> Bulldozed by Luther and Weyerhauser . . .
>
> Trees down
> Creeks choked, trout killed, roads.

The leading figure of Protestantism links up directly to the modern corporation, as if Weber's *The Protestant Ethic and the Spirit of Capitalism* was correct but took too long to make its points. Throughout the Western tradition, early and late, hardy, decadent, or theocratic, the impulse to denude nature has remained unflagging. Snyder's guilt at this sort of exploitation turns into cynicism, and he resents the "meaningless / abstractions of the educated mind" and even finds a fitting image for his attitude of rejection:

> Drop a mouthful of useless words.
> —The book's in the crapper
> They're up to the part on Ethics now

Out of this dismissal of traditional Western ethics Snyder will try to forge his new myth, but this first section of the book deals with logging in another sense, namely the activity of clearing the ground for new growth. In the second and third sections we begin to see the positive and negative aspects of different metaphorical activities.

In the book's middle section, "Hunting," Snyder explores the power-vision of solitude and invokes the shamanistic techniques of hunting, in which the hunter cultivates a primitive consciousness akin to animism. The poet will

> sit without thoughts by the log-road
> Hatching a new myth
> watching the waterdogs
> the last truck gone.

In the wilderness cleared of the exploiters of natural resources, a different temporal order reasserts itself. Here moments of intense awareness become possible, man can again "believe his own senses." This is Snyder's poetic at its most immanent, finding its orders and stabilities in heightened sensory awareness and empathetic powers. This order most resembles the world of those nature poems in *Riprap,* though here Snyder seems more willing to let the thematic point of the poem declare itself:

> First day of the world.
> White rock ridges
> new born
> Jay chatters the first time
> Rolling a smoke by the campfire
> New! never before.

This recalls the sense of Wordsworth's "Westminster Bridge" sonnet, with its claim that "Never did sun more beautifully steep / In his first splendour, valley, rock, or hill." Of course at this point Wordsworth is comparing natural beauty to the even higher beauty of the urban scene before him—an uncharacteristic moment for him, and one we can assume Snyder would not fully endorse. But the sense of the primal, original temporality serves as the mediation for both poets, as a way out of the spoilage of man's history without abandoning the glories of nature's processes. But the "new myth" of the first poem in this section is understood best, I think, as the coming synthesis of Buddhism and Amerindian thought, for it is in the second and third sections of *Myths & Texts* that Snyder begins to reimagine and remetaphorize his cosmic and political visions. The Buddha and Coyote will begin to replace the idiom of Western political thought that dominates, say, the Roman imagery of Wordsworth's political sonnets. But as with Eliot's "The Fire Sermon" in *The Waste Land,* the reigning value is neither exclusively Western nor Eastern, but a master term—*compassion* or *love*—that surmounts the ethical system of both world views. The section ends with a poem about the Buddha, here conceived as a symbolic fullness of the natural order, as animals come and offer him milk and nuts and he is seen as "drunk / On wine or truth, what you will, / meaning: compassion." The agents of this compassion are man and beast, and all the "beasts / got the buddha-nature." All but Coyote, that is, as Snyder uses this figure as his bridge to the next section.

For the figure of Coyote in Snyder's writings we have to turn to *The Old Ways,* where in one essay he discusses Coyote as both a trickster figure and a mythic figure who is responsible for death in the world. As Kali ended the first section of *Myths & Texts,* smashing the order of commodified time with the larger forces of cosmic time, so Coyote ends the middle section by interjecting into the heightened awareness of a sort of pastoral realm the harder questions of the void. The final section, "Burning," is Snyder's meditation on evil and nothingness, and it is his confrontation with a temporal order that stretches beyond, and yet includes, world history. Eventually the resolution to the threat of nothingness comes in the form of art—"Poetry a riprap on the slick rock of metaphysics," as he puts it, referring to that cobble of stones used to form trails in the mountain wilderness. The section begins with a shaman's song but moves on to poems about the void and the "endless changing hell, / Life and death whipped /

On this froth of reality." At one point Coyote returns to say, "I guess there never was a world anywhere," but he is answered by a figure called "Earthmaker," who says, "I think if we find a little world, / I can fix it up." This tension between the playful nihilism of Coyote and the ameliorative cosmology of Earthmaker forms one of the overriding struggles in both this section and the whole book, and even throughout all of Snyder's work. A belief in art, as an imaginative resolution of tensions or as the preservation and restoration of lost and threatened values, concluded the first section, "Logging," with these lines: "The brush / may paint the mountains and streams / Though the territory is lost." We will see below just how the artistic vision parallels and informs the political vision.

The social and political dimensions of experience are present in "Burning," but there they take up some of the characteristics of the void and are strongly influenced by Buddhist thought. In section 12, for example, Snyder speaks of the "city of the Gandharvas," which is "not a real city" but

> Only the memory of a city
> Preserved in seed from beginningless time.
>   a city crowded with books,
> Thick grass on the streets,
>   a race of dark people
> Wearing thin sandals, reading all morning in alleys
> Glazing black pots at night.

This city exists in history, but only virtually, as the idea of a city, as the poems in *Riprap* presented the idea of the family unit. Echoes from Eliot's *The Waste Land*, with its "unreal city," suggest themselves, but for Eliot the city is cosmopolitan, cultured, and historically significant: Athens, Jerusalem, London. For Snyder, the city remains almost a natural process ("Preserved in seed"), and its culture remains somewhat primitive, though supported by texts that presumably embody traditional and developed values. In typical Buddhist paradox, the urban ideal exists as both a memory and a historical fulfillment to be struggled toward. The Gandharvas are heavenly musicians, and so there is also the irony that the city of the Gandharvas is figuratively an illusion.[7]

This brings us to one of the key themes of "Burning," derived from Snyder's Buddhist readings and also drawing on his knowledge of Amerindian lore. Put simply, this theme would argue that the physical world might be treated as an illusion, but it is an illusion that must be worked with and worked through. To move quickly or casually past the physical dimension would lead to an insufficient understanding of the total process. A key incident that illustrates this comprises section 8 of "Burning," where Snyder recounts a story about John Muir, the naturalist. While climbing Mount Ritter, Muir became trapped and felt that his doom "appeared fixed"; then, however, he experienced something like the rearrangement of the mental field that William James described in *Varieties of Religious Experience,* and a new form of vision presented itself:

> My mind seemed to fill with a
> Stifling smoke. This terrible eclipse
> Lasted only a moment, when life blazed
> Forth again in preternatural clearness.
> I seemed suddenly to become possessed
> Of a new sense. My trembling muscles
> Became firm again, every rift and flaw in
> The rocks was seen as through a microscope,
> My limbs moved with a positiveness and precision
> With which I seemed to have
> Nothing at all to do.

The image of smoke forms a connection with the other images of the void that occur throughout "Burning" (along with images of foam and froth—recall the frail "foam" from "T-2 Tanker Blues" in *Riprap*). But Muir's experience demonstrates that the insubstantiality need not be final and that the "seer" is returned to a world of perceptual energy and clarity. Note, too, how here the "every rift and flaw" recalls the granite of *Riprap*'s title poem, with its

7. I draw here, and in other places, on *Some Notes to Gary Snyder's Myths & Texts,* by Howard McCord (Berkeley: Sand Dollar, 1971).

"crystal and sediment linked hot / all change," and as the control of the individual subject dissipates or is taken away, another, larger force appears and begins to sustain and energize the environment.

The transformation of perceptual energies at the level of the individual must be met by an analogous transformation on the political level. In section 6 of "Burning," Snyder recalls "The motto in the Wobbly hall," where the International Workers of the World (the IWW, known by the nickname *Wobblies*) held their meetings. The motto was the Marxist idea of "Forming the New Society / Within the shell of the Old," and Snyder's own early political consciousness, which he has described as "beginning with his parents' 'socialist-radical' views and developing into a politics that was "Marxist, Anarchist, and onwards," here found a rich and fitting image.[8] The shell, of course, recalls the "seed" of the Gandharvas' city, and the dialectic of "forming" and re-forming contains an organicist understanding that correlates with natural processes. Such a correlation between natural and political processes reaches back to Coleridge and his organicism, and even further back to the medieval notion of the king's two bodies. What makes Snyder's use of the correlation distinctive is the emphasis on personal transformation as a kind of mediation between nature and the political or social realm. Snyder's use of the void might easily be misread as only a way of justifying the Buddhist negation of will, but I think it is more correctly seen as a way of recontextualizing political vision. Without a theocentric justification for hierarchy and other structures of authority, the best grounding for modern political thought is in an understanding of nature, its powers and limitations. This point of view, however, relies on a nature different from that defined by

8. Any number of passages from Marx could serve as the ground of the Wobblies' slogan. But one from "The Civil War in France" is especially germane: "They [the working class] have no ideals to realize but to set free the elements of the new society with which old collapsing bourgeois society itself is pregnant." However, right before this sentence there is a passage that speaks of the need to pass "through long struggles." See *Karl Marx, On Revolution,* ed. Saul K. Padover (New York: McGraw Hill, 1971), p. 353.

Newtonian physics or modern technology. It is also a nature different from that of the romantic poets, but clearly it is closer to their nature than to that of the entrepreneurs who control the logging industry of the Pacific northwest. Nature must include the void as *its* ultimate ground.

Beyond the historical realm the cosmic order lies, churning in dialectical union and opposition, and this dialectic can in turn generate historical and political paradox. Nowhere is this paradox greater than when Snyder contrasts the bringing of Buddhism into China with "Lenin in a sealed train through Germany," the one a "surrender into freedom," the other a "revolt into slavery." But both historical events are ultimately illusory, man's self-born mockery of his own enterprise. The "middle of the universe" can as well be a lookout station in a national forest as anywhere else. What is demanded finally is a sense of personal, idealized awareness of "Buddha incense in an empty world." "Rain falls for centuries," as we are told in the poem's last section, "soaking the loose rocks in space," and the individual experience of a forest fire in the Skagit valley of the Pacific Northwest becomes a symbol of the cosmic fire of the universe—the text, or sensory experience, turns into a myth, or imaginative construct. Snyder accepts the void as he accepts the forest fire; in other words, he sees human history as little more than the "last wisp of smoke [that] floats up / Into the absolute cold." The poem concludes with Thoreau's line, "The sun is but a morning star," which here refers to something like the speculative cosmology of Eastern thought that imagines the universe destroyed and re-created in a constant cycle that is both illusory and unlimited. Snyder's personal voice preempts history by transsuming it into a moment of heightened consciousness. But Snyder's grounding myth must be read as Rich's mythic woman was read, that is, as a way of seeing the political in some larger context. Neither Rich nor Snyder sees political structures or values as ultimate, but both see that politics must be rightly ordered if the ultimate values are to be recognized and preserved.

Another way to view the structure of *Myths & Texts* is to use the idea of turning an earth into a world and, conversely, of discovering the earth in the world. I am using these two terms with the meaning conferred on them in Heidegger's essay "The Origin of the Work of Art." There, *earth* is defined as the ground on which man bases his dwelling, a place of sheltering and enclosure. *World*, on the other hand, is defined in part negatively, as other than the "mere collection" of things or the "imagined framework" of such things. Instead, Heidegger sees the world as a process (he speaks of how "the world worlds"), a nonobjective condition and activity that has "a necessity and a nearness of its own." Though analogous to the terms *nature* and *culture*, *earth* and *world* are, especially in the work of art, seen as dialectically intertwined, each struggling for domination of the other, while at the same time providing both the possibility and the limits of the other. Here is the passage that sets out their relationship:

> The world is the self-disclosing openness of the broad paths of the simple and essential decisions in the destiny of an historical people. The earth is the spontaneous forthcoming of that which is continually self-secluding and to that extent sheltering and concealing. World and earth are essentially different from one another and yet are never separated. The world grounds itself on the earth, and earth juts through world. But the relation between world and earth does not wither away into the empty unity of opposites unconcerned with one another. The world, in resting upon the earth, strives to surmount it. As self-opening it cannot endure anything closed. The earth, however, as sheltering and concealing, tends always to draw the world into itself and keep it there.

If we regard the boundaries between earth and world as shifting forms of interactive energies, then many of the poems in *Myths & Texts* can be read as outlining the folds and contours of these boundaries. Here is a passage from the second poem of the "Burning" section.

> One moves continually with the consciousness
> Of that other, totally alien, non-human:

Humming inside like a taut drum,
Carefully avoiding any direct thought of it,
Attentive to the real-world flesh and stone.
Intricate layers of emptiness
This only world, juggling forms
  a hand, a breast, two clasped
Human tenderness scuttles
Down dry endless cycles
Forms within forms falling
                clinging
Loosely, what's gone away?
          —love

This passage owes a good deal to the metaphoric entanglement of erotic drive and the regeneration of the natural growth cycle, as is made clear in the lines just beyond this passage, and it even echoes distantly such poems as Pound's Canto 47, where this metaphor is explored in depth. But I would identify the "alien, non-human" realm with Heidegger's *earth*, and the realm of "flesh and stone" with that of *world*. In a sense, the phrase "This only world" would be the dialectical union of these two realms, for Snyder, like Heidegger, is very concerned to overcome any subject-object split that would sever the conscious ego from the environment of its daily experience. But there persists for Snyder another dimension, the ineffable energy and presence of natural forces, that always threatens to establish its own dominion; as Heidegger puts it, "earth juts through world."

The political dimension is involved here because of "the essential decisions in the destiny of an historical people" that Heidegger sees as being made possible by the structuring of the world. Snyder's view of the political destiny of America is in large part shaped by a sense that the world has too forcefully dominated the earth. In its rush to a technological and industrial society, the American spirit in the nineteenth century was willing to suppress or ignore the supporting force of the environment it was bent on exploiting. This phenomenon was perhaps most striking in the American West, and in discussing the literature of the West (in the essay "The Incredible Survival of

Coyote" in *The Old Ways*), Snyder proposes a historical explanation.

> The usual literature of the West is concerned with the period of exploitation and expansion west of the tree line. . . . A period of expansion, first-phase exploitation. It is not a literature of place. It's a history and a literature of feats of strength and of human events. . . . It's only about this place by accident. . . . Anglos from temperate climates suddenly confronted with vast, treeless, arid spaces. . . . The West, then, presented us with an image of manliness, of vigor, of courage, of humor, of heroics which became a very strong part of our national self-image; perhaps the strongest part, the most pervasive, the one which has been most exported to the rest of the world.

Snyder consciously realizes that this image of the West does not tell the whole story of the American experience. But just as clearly he realizes that the land Americans first settled, east of the Mississippi, was a land that produced a political vision that made the "first-phase exploitation" of the West possible and even desirable. One of the traditional political values of the early theorists of the American republic was to husband the small individual farm with its focus on what Leo Marx has called the "middle landscape." Jeffersonian pastoralism, in this view, praises certain primitive values, especially rugged independence and an abhorrence of urban life and institutions. But Jefferson's ideals do not demand total primitivism, and they are the product of a rational, Enlightenment commitment to balance and an ordered polity. But we could also see his ideals as enunciating a state where world and earth are in harmony; indeed, there is a distinctly aesthetic sense about the pastoralism contained in query 19 of the *Notes on Virginia*.

The historical irony, of course, comes when this independent spirit is sundered from the "middle landscape" Jefferson praised and is set against the very different environment of the West. In another essay from *The Old Ways*, "The Politics of Ethnopoetics," Snyder addresses the problem of what occurs when "small, relatively self-sufficient cultures begin to contact each other and that interaction becomes stepped up by a historical process of growing populations, growing accumulation of surplus wealth and so forth." Clearly the question of the size of a cultural or political grouping becomes crucial for Snyder, since the scale of desires and conflicts in advanced industrial society makes images of natural harmony less forceful in determining consciousness and action. Eventually Snyder is forced to conclude that "maybe" the arms race began with the bronze age; in this case we are close to the myth of original sin, a myth that Snyder by and large avoids in his work. He then offers a distinction between cultures that must protect their environment and its ecosystem, because it provides, directly, their economic base, and other cultures that "spread their economic support system out far enough that they can afford to wreck one ecosystem, and keep moving on." Essentially this latter is Snyder's description of imperialism, which he sees as having operated in ancient Rome and Babylon as well as in modern America. He connects this destructiveness with the "centralized state" and also with slavery, which he sees as an exploitation of energy that is necessitated by, and dialectically provides the means for, a growth in consumption. The political vision of Snyder, like that of Jefferson, rests on a sense of scale that was toppled by the onrush of nineteenth-century industrialization. Jefferson's vision looks backward to the landed gentry of the eighteenth century, where an almost feudal sense of land-based political values was sedimented in the growing institutions of mercantile capitalism. Snyder's vision looks forward to a politics where smaller units of social identity can reestablish connections with the earth even as they sustain an order that rests on a worldwide sense of values. *Myths & Texts* is the work in which many of Snyder's political reflections first take clear shape. Despite the book's greater complexity in this area than, say, *Riprap,* the problems are by no means settled. What comes next for Snyder is a not only sharper but also more troubled sense of both nature and the political realm.

II. Figures

> He rated it as a gain in coming to America, that here you
> could get tea, and coffee, and meat every day. But the only
> true America is that country where you are at liberty to pur-
> sue such a mode of life as may enable you to do without
> these.
>
> —Thoreau

Before looking at the next volumes in Snyder's career, I
want to suggest some ways of reading his poetry by offering models for the various kinds of lyric structures the
books contain. We have already seen the model of
"riprap," poetry made dense and objectlike and yet containing the possibility of energized transitions to other
states of awareness. Another model is the haiku; some of
Snyder's poems are written and labeled as such, but others borrow from the techniques of haiku and combine
these borrowings with traditional Western lyric structures.
I will discuss a few of Snyder's haiku in the context of *The
Back Country* and so will say little here, except to note that
the haiku and the "riprap" models are closely related.
Snyder has compared poetry writing to backpacking, that
is, it involves recognizing the minimum limit of one's
needs in order to travel light; the goal is the process itself,
the movement, and not the trappings. There is at least a
subjective connection here to a reaction against commodity fetishism. In Marxist terms, the commodity is
fetishized when its exchange value far outstrips its use
value. In the economical language of a Snyder poem, use
value is elevated over exchange value. Such a connection
will strike many as fanciful, and by itself it will not stand
intense analytic scrutiny. Seen in the context of Snyder's
general condemnation of the waste and falsely stimulated
appetites of the capitalist order, however, I think the connection is more valid. But someone might as convincingly
argue that Snyder fetishizes words themselves, profiling
their dense materiality in a way cognate with the focused

and obsessive concern of an acquisitive capitalist collector, if not consumer. No such one-to-one correspondence between political vision and artistic forms is readily acceptable, of course, and one has always to remember that forms can be used with a variety of contents (as any parodist knows), despite what some formalist critics would have us believe.

Still, the intuitive connection dies hard. Another model for Snyder's poems is the rhythm he experienced during the job he worked at while a poem was being conceived. Here's how he put it, in the essay he contributed to Donald Allen's anthology, *The New American Poetry: 1945 – 1960:* "I've just recently come to realize that the rhythms of my poems follow the rhythm of physical work I'm doing and life I'm leading at any given time—which makes the music in my head which creates the line."

Though he does not offer it as such, this might well be the description of a true proletarian art such as the writers of the 1930s searched for, in vain as it happens. But to fulfill this ideal genuinely we would be forced to modify, or perhaps just minimize, the implications of that last phrase. If the rhythm has to be mediated by the mind before it shapes the line, how can we be sure false consciousness won't warp it? This brings us to a truism—but a powerful truth nonetheless—that we cannot expect to have a socialist art (or an anarchic one) without a socialist political order. Art forms can contain or express *past* social realities (though often with diminished force),but they cannot fully embody *future* social values. Perhaps the best Snyder can do, that any writer can do, is to work with the possibilities of figurative language and artistic form currently available, trying by these very figures to both embody and *dis*-embody the political world he envisions.

This impulse, to contain the vision in a figure or to use the figure to point beyond the reality, is clearly an ambivalent one, and Snyder does not escape the ambiguities it leaves in its wake. Pointing beyond: this is a gesture of the anarchists and the chiliasts, that group of revolutionary medieval spiritualists who first enunciated radical political ideals as a part of their religious dissent. (They will come up again in the discussion of *Earth House Hold*.) But pointing beyond is also a gesture associated with the haiku, surrounded as it traditionally was in Oriental literature with a complex semantic code of strictures and expectations about measure, subject matter, and virtually every aesthetic feature. Yet this structure was what provided for, and we might say was defeated by, the air of spontaneity that remained the sine qua non of the form. To satisfy all the requirements and yet to overleap the bounds remains a figural equation that attracts many writers, not all of whom solve it. With political structures, at least this much of an analogy may be permissible: the area between theory and praxis is always the area of greatest interest, and greatest struggle.

For a context to Snyder's claim that the rhythm of the poem is figured by the rhythm of physical activity, we can turn to another revolutionary poet (if not a poet-revolutionary), in one of his most challenging arguments. Here is Wordsworth, in the "Preface" to the *Lyrical Ballads:*

> Humble and rustic life was generally chosen, because in that condition the essential passions of the heart find a better soil in which they can attain their maturity . . . and, lastly, because in that condition the passions of men are incorporated with the beautiful and permanent forms of nature.

Add to this Keats's insistence that poetry had better come to him as naturally as the leaves to a tree or it had better not come at all, and we can see Snyder's attempt as part of the larger post-Enlightenment desire to naturalize the form of the aesthetic object. But what of Snyder's rhythms of the mechanical turbine that powers the oil tanker on which he is a sailor (as we will see in a poem called "Oil," from *The Back Country*)? Would this constitute a beautiful and permanent form of nature? Hardly—yet Snyder's rhythm would at least be personalized, if not naturalized in the romantic sense. This tying of the poem to a bodily process becomes the impulse that most shapes the meter-making argument of which Emerson spoke.

Eventually Snyder will propose a poetics of the breath, and a poetics of wave motion and periodicity, as the source of his poetry's array of rhythmic shapes and rhetorical figures. Both breath and wave require a physical component to be actualized, though each can be thought of as an abstract pattern. In this they resemble the vortex that Hugh Kenner expertly analyzed in *The Pound Era*. But as a figure for the poem's energy, that is, as a metaphor for the very shape of a poetic structure, breath and wave finally enable Snyder to both personalize and communalize his vision. Again, a reading of Snyder continually raises the question of how far can aesthetic means embody or express a political vision, and in what terms? Are we not conditioned to reading all aesthetic statements and experiences as nonpurposive, contemplative, shapely but without intention to act on or alter social reality? Can a poem make us refigure our social and political myths and master terms? Can the poet use the poem to show us the shapeliness of mind and so call us back from our weary despairs and on to some utopian harmony, made not only *like* but *of* a communalized and lyric equity of consciousness? Consider this formulation by Georg Simmel, from *The Conflict in Modern Culture and Other Essays* (the "here" is presumably Germany in 1896, the date of the essay, and a country Simmel describes as "characterized by heterogeneous interests and irreconcilable tendencies"):

> A socialistic and balanced society through its organic unity, its symmetrical arrangement and mutual coordination of movements in common centers, provides for the observing mind a maximum of insight. To understand the social picture here requires a minimum of intellectual effort. This fact in its aesthetic significance would seem to figure decisively in the intellectual appeal of socialism.
>
> In aesthetics, symmetry means the dependence of individual elements on their mutual interdependence with all others, but also self-containment within the designated circle. Asymmetrical arrangements permit broader individual rights, more latitude for the free and far-reaching relations of each element. The internal organization of socialism takes this into consideration; thus it is no accident that all historical approximations to socialism occurred only within strictly closed groups which declined all relations to outside powers.

As Wordsworth tries to naturalize the aesthetic, so Simmel tries to aestheticize the political. In doing so he implicitly argues that socialism must deny or curtail "individual rights." On this point, Snyder's political vision argues precisely the opposite, for he believes that only by expanding individual consciousness and activity can society be made truly harmonious and beautiful. Doubtlessly Simmel would differ with Snyder about aesthetic matters as well as on political issues. That either could convince the other of a political point by appealing to an aesthetic figure is as unlikely as the reverse. But if the aesthetic and the political are not analogues of one another, why do they so often hold their ground in such similar ways? The tradition in which Simmel argues might be identified as neo-Kantian. Recalling Kant's triad of works, in which the metaphysical, the moral, and the aesthetic realms are addressed, we can see that for Simmel the aesthetic realm must be somehow cognate with other forms of truth, that our sense of beauty is a guide to our senses of truth or justice, and vice versa. Simmel goes on to argue that our aesthetic sense in modern society is extraordinarily broad and can be connected to "the most opposite poles of social interest," that is, we can see as aesthetically pleasing political arrangements that either stress or deny the importance of the individual. Furthermore, the opposing aesthetic styles of "naturalism" and "formalism," though the first aims for closeness to objects and the second insists on placing postulates about beauty and significance between us and objects, have an important trait in common. Simmel sees all modern art as trying to separate us from our familiarity with the world, to create distance (here the announced aims of naturalism are paradoxically reversed), and this fragmented, distanced world is the result of "the steadily deeper penetration of a money economy," which interrupts the "immediacy of impression" and thereby weakens our "active interest" in things. What is interesting about Simmel's argument is not so much its demonstrable truth or error; it is the philosopher's need to find a figure of thought that will enable him to see the social and the aesthetic realms in one term, or in a set of terms.

Much of this "mixing of realms" is the result of the traditions of Western European discourse, though certain similarities exist in the East as well, as the example of Confucius shows. I raise the issue, obviously not to resolve it or even with any hope of clarifying it, but only to place at or near the center of any reading of Snyder the problem of figurative language. More specifically, I think we have at least to ask if the poet's master terms or controlling myths are aesthetic in origin and then (perhaps mistakenly) applied to the political realm, or the other way around. There might also be the possibility that what Snyder is after, and his success is best measured against just such a possibility, is a figure that will allow him to see the aesthetic and the political not only with equal accuracy but also with equal validity. Another version of this possibility would thus see his syncretism of cultural values not as an evasion of political rigor but rather as the best way to reimagine both the poetic and the political. Some of these questions might be brought into focus by looking at Snyder's writings of the 1960s.

The Back Country

With its four sections—"Far West," "Far East," "Kali," and "Back"—*The Back Country* possesses a clear overall structure. If we realize the fourth section refers, among other things, to a return to America, and if we recognize in "Kali" that much of the imagery and incidents are drawn from Snyder's visit to India in 1962, then obviously place becomes the central metaphor of the book. Place, conceived as environment and the ground of cultural and imaginative life, serves as one of the main sources of value and wisdom throughout Snyder's work. But in *The Back Country* we have more than the figurative transformation of place into consciousness, we also have what is perhaps (except for *Riprap*) Snyder's least political volume. I would suggest that much of *The Back Country* is protopolitical, that is, that Snyder sees in the places of the book the generally negative effects of political systems. Additionally, the book explores that sense of place that endures beyond, or rises above, political structures. For me a telling passage comes in "The Firing," a poem from the "Far East" section, where the "riprap" description of the firing of pottery in a kiln celebrates an almost sacred act of community, one that produces objects both serviceable and transcendent:

> The hands you layed on clay
> Kickwheeled, curling,
>   creamed to the lip of nothing,
> and coaxt to a white dancing heat that day
> Will linger centuries in these towns and loams
> And speak to men or beasts
> When Japanese and English
> Are dead tongues.

The potter's artifact endures beyond national identities as a form of communication to and with both animal and human orders, and we can also see in this passage two other figures that will become important for all of *The Back Country:* "nothing" and "dancing." As I hope to demonstrate, the "Kali" section resembles the "Burning" section of *Riprap,* for it revolves around Snyder's confrontation with destruction and nihilism. But "Back" resolves the negative tones that threaten to dominate all of the volume and does so by turning to figures of sensual completion and harmony, for which the epitome is the figure of graceful movement or dance. In the largest terms, *The Back Country* serves as a spiritual autobiography, tracing Snyder's life through some of his darkest hours and finally driving through to the limits of his fear and his desires, back to a more stable and rooted sense of integrity and acceptance.

The focus on the nonpolitical begins with the first poem in "Far West," which deals with the figure of Coyote, the "smooth loper / Crapulous old man, a drifter," who stands for all the socially unacceptable values and forms of consciousness. The poem concludes with Coyote observing the city on the one hand and the wilderness on the other. In the wilderness he sees "People gone, no disaster," and when looking to the social realm he observes a "Dead city in dry summer." Celebrating wilderness is part of the tradition of the literature of the American West, and such political vision as is explicit in this kind of celebration is rampantly individualistic, with little chance or even desire for a future or for a corrective reintegration with large populations. This is not Thoreau's notion that "in wilderness is the preservation of the world" so much as it is a cry of the beast against any order that would limit personal freedom. The spirit of Huck Finn and Kesey's McMurphy assumes dominance throughout much of this section of the book. But even here Snyder's awareness extends beyond a merely negative or renunciatory gesture. He has seen the political order and its dominance from the underside as well as the outside and thus appreciates the near totality of its power. Here is a poem that shows a heightened consciousness that cannot yet conceive of a transcendent solution:

OIL

soft rainsqualls on the swells
south of the Bonins, late at night. Light
from the empty mess-hall
throws back bulky shadows
of winch and fairlead
over the slanting fantail where I stand.

but for men on watch in the engine room,
the man at the wheel, the lookout in the bow,
the crew sleeps. in cots on deck
or narrow iron bunks down drumming
passageways below.

the ship burns with a furnace heart
steam veins and copper nerves
quivers and slightly twists and always goes—
easy roll of the hull and deep
vibration of the turbine underfoot.

bearing what all these
crazed, hooked nations need:
steel plates and
long injections of pure oil.

The anthropomorphizing of the ship represents Snyder's only way to give power a sufficiently vivid figuration, and the explicit image of addiction (or at least medical care) in the last lines of the poem manages faintly to humanize and yet harshly criticize the system of industrial growth and "technological drivenness." The men who tend the system have little hope for escape or surcease, since even as they sleep the ship "quivers and slightly twists and always goes." Motion and haptic awareness, the roll and vibration, the drumming, all become unnatural in their ongoingness, their lack of periodicity. The other poems in this section celebrate a consciousness that knows a mix of freedom and necessity, even if the freedom is circumscribed or merely latent, but this poem's sense of entrapment will resurface in other sections, especially "Kali."

The short poem "Burning the small dead" has been analyzed by Charles Altieri,[1] who has shown how it served Snyder's need to create models of consciousness that can serve as adequate reflections of the immanent, orderly forces of nature that allow it, nature, to become not only a source of harmony but also the ultimate ground of value. Here is the entire poem:

> Burning the small dead
>   branches
> broke from beneath
>   thick spreading
>   whitebark pine.
>
>   A hundred summers
> Snowmelt rock and air
> hiss in a twisted bough.
>
>   sierra granite;
>   mt. Ritter—
>   black rock twice as old.
>
> Deneb, Altair
>
> windy fire

1. In *Enlarging the Temple,* pp. 137–38.

I will not attempt to recapitulate all of Altieri's superbly sensitive reading, except to say that, as Snyder moves from dead organic matter to an active transformation and on to distant celestial bodies, summing all the products and processes in the very image—"windy fire"—that also serves as a metaphor for the consciousness that links them, the implicit figuration builds on a haiku-like poetics that reaches far beyond the limited imagism of, say, the early Williams. What I would like to do is to propose that the notion of the poem as a model of consciousness, in which figurative language serves as the container of the objects and the energies they embody as well as the mental states that the poem releases and records, can serve for all the poems in *The Back Country*. Thus we can move to the complex figure of the kiva that closes the final section of the book from the limited figurative energy of an actual haiku, in the sequence "Hitch Haiku" in the "Far West" section. This contrasts the wastefulness of industrial society with the immensity of natural scenes, in this case a chasm in the floor of the ocean:

Over the Mindanao Deep

Scrap brass
    dumpt off the fantail
falling six miles

The wasted material is almost renaturalized as we picture its leaflike tumble and fall through a different medium; the world of objects never completely loses its transformative energies. In most of the cases, however, *The Back Country* uses a meditative sensibility almost exclusively, and the observing subject of the book's center proceeds with a self-awareness that often avoids transformation in favor of comprehension.

In the "Far East" section Snyder is very much the émigré, haunted by memories of home and, though stimulated by a new culture, less and less able to formulate a vision that will lift the horizon of his concerns. The "Far East" begins with a poem that shows Snyder's inept physical skills as "Old Mrs. Kawabata" is able to harvest "more in two hours" than he can manage in a day. Yet the poem ends with the old woman putting "five dusty stalks / of ragged wild blue flower" in a jar to brighten the poet's kitchen. This displacement of the practical with the aesthetic becomes the controlling figure for the entire section. But this theme is complicated by another: the haunting by memory. Snyder is unable to shed his Occidental values, and nowhere is this more painfully shown than in "Four Poems for Robin." Here Snyder tells of the inextinguishable pain of the relationship he had with his first wife, Alison, whose nickname is Robin. Clearly he wants to achieve a Zen-like sense of calm and acceptance in regard to ineradicable but unalterable experience, but the demons of self-doubt and ego are not easily denied:

> We had what the others
> All crave and seek for;
> We left it behind at nineteen.
>
> I feel ancient as though I had
> Lived many lives.
>
> And may never now know
> If I am a fool
> Or have done what my
>   karma demands.

The ancient feeling could be a Zen-like achievement, representing the negation of the will and the extension of a temporal scale that therapeutically resolves the sense of self-recrimination. But it could equally be a figuration for spiritual and emotional exhaustion and futility. The last stanza only reiterates this fundamental ambivalence. Much of "Far East" can be read as a sort of pained or naive questioning of social identity, brought about ostensibly by the exposure to a new culture but also unconsciously dramatizing the questioning of individual identity. The section ends with a long poem, "Six Years," which summarizes Snyder's stay in Japan by using the structure of the twelve months of the year. This condensation of a long period into one ordered "metatemporal" unit allows the poet to organize and reduce his myriad observations and reactions to a "foreign" land, and so the poem serves as the log of a metaphoric acculturation. But the "Envoy to Six Years," the final part of the sequence, shows us Snyder in the "belly of the ship," headed back to America. Much of what Snyder learned in Japan is spelt out more explicitly in the prose essays of *Earth House Hold*. The "Six Years" sequence offers little thematic clarity and is, to my mind, successful only as a picture, not an interpretation, of another society and its culture.

The last two sections of *The Back Country* contain some of Snyder's most tentative poetry, in which his attempts to structure the affective and intellectual models of his experience alternate between large forceful statements and brief, evanescent images. In "Far East" Snyder blurted out the feeling of "To hell with all these cultures—history / after the Jurassic is a bore." In "Kali," we are first presented with a memory of Alison, who "whimpered all night long / with evil dreams," and then with poems with titles like "To Hell with Your Fertility Cult" and "Wandering the Old, Dirty Countries." The chief, though not sole or dominant, tone is one of rejection, and it is strongest in a poem like "This Tokyo," which begins with these lines:

Peace, war, religion
Revolution will not help.
This horror seeds in the agile
Thumb and greedy little brain
That learned to catch bananas
With a stick
    The millions of us worthless
To each other or the world
Or selves, the sufferers of the real
Or of the mind—this world
Is but a dream?

"This Tokyo" ends over a page later by repeating the opening sentence. The clear implication is that the evolutionary process itself, with the development of the opposing thumb and the rise of the primates, contains the seeds of all the evil of the industrialized world. Nowhere else in all of Snyder's work is he so bleakly hopeless, though in

57

other poems in this section, like "Xrist" and "The Man-ichaeans," he comes close. Near the end of the section the spirit lifts, though an elegiac strain persists. An elegy for John Chappell, one of the potters who figured in "The Firing," and a few poems celebrating sexual passion provide a feeling of resolution, and the section ends with a fairly traditional treatment of the subject of psychic rebirth, including these closing lines in which, significantly, the poet addresses himself in the third person; the "you" here is the Mother, in part the eternal feminine, and in part the principle of fecundity:

> Snyder says: you bear me, nurse me
> I meet you, always love you,
> > you dance
> > on my chest and thigh
>
> Forever born again.

The image of the dance triumphs over the images of nothingness that are more numerous, and the final sense of the section relies on Indian cosmology, with the Hindu goddesses of destruction and rebirth dancing in an endless alternation of death and fertility. Snyder traces these principles to the pulses of his body, and so the focus remains on the individual values and experience.

"Back" includes several overtly political poems, though they tend to be resolved with images of contemplation, or even playfulness. The most striking is perhaps "To the Chinese Comrades," in which the early promise of the Cultural Revolution apparently had not yet turned sour. In this poem, Snyder weaves together personal reflections of his early experiences of Chinese people—learning to use chopsticks in a Chinese restaurant in Portland when he was twenty-one, with a student's fervor for revolutionary ideas ("holding hands, kissing / in the evening talkt Lenin and Marx"), as well as a sort of comic dream-vision where Mao and Khrushchev face each other "across a wide plain" and the confrontation ends with good-natured laughter. The poem concludes with Snyder advising Chairman Mao to quit smoking, "Build dams, plant trees, / don't kill flies by hand." He goes on, in fact, to urge the revolutionary leader to "Write some poems. Swim the river . . . Don't shoot me, let's go drinking. / just / wait." The whole poem reads like a political statement made by someone who mistrusts politics; though it reflects the air of delight and spontaneity many felt was redolent in the heyday of the revolutionary sixties, it does not wholly avoid elements of humorous condescension and escapism. The spirit of Kerouac at his most insouciant colors the poem's political vision.

This poem is followed by "For the West," another jeu d'esprit on the theme of revolution that relies on fanciful and mythical figures, so that Europe comes out as "Europa," "a woman's counting," and America shows forth as

> the flowery glistening oil blossom
>   spreading on water—
> it was so tiny, nothing, now it keeps expanding
> all those colors,
>   our world
>   opening inside outward toward us,
> each part swelling and turning
> who would have thought such turning.

Here the conceit is intended to configure the industrial overtones of an oil slick with the Dantesque connotations of a transcendent, all embracing flower, but the firm clarity of a poem like "Oil" is lost. Ending with a claim of personal insight ("I see down again through clear water") and the evocation of a "rhyme the / little girl was singing," the larger dimensions of the poem, never very clear or original, fade off into "fantastic patterns," essentially contemplative or aesthetic images.

Some of the poems in this last section, such as "August Was Foggy" and "Beneath My Hand and Eye the Distant Hills, Your Body," celebrate "new rain" and the vision of landscape joined with the erotic body of the lover and "loving what it feeds on." But I think "Through the Smoke Hole" stands as the most complex poem in "Back," and it is the penultimate poem in the book as well (excepting the translations of Miyazawa Kenji, a modern Japanese poet with at least some vague resemblance to the Han-shan of the "Cold Mountain Poems" in *Riprap*). "Through the Smoke Hole" imagines a ceremony in the kiva, the early Amerindian structure (many of which were unearthed in Chaco Canyon in New Mexico, part of an elaborate Hohokam culture that predated that of the Hopi and Navaho), with its domed roof and smoke hole, which served as the cosmological imagery through which religious rituals enacted dramas of spiritual migration and transformation. Snyder envisions two "worlds"; the space above the smoke hole, and the space below the ground of the kiva. Altogether, there are four routes, since it is possible to travel in both directions along the path to the world above and to the world below. Men come up from below as dream images or demons; they go down below into a kind of death. Men disappear up as "great heros shining through the smoke"; individuals return from above as transformed spirits or totemic animals, chief among them Coyote. The kiva, and its magic highway of smoke, thus becomes the world of unborn nature, procreative nature, and even human society. It is the great metaphoric figure that enables Snyder to mediate between the dark forces of the unconscious mind and the necessary understanding of nature that will allow the society to survive in a harsh environment. The kiva is the center of the imagined, mythical universe, and the last lines of the poem, "plain men / come out of the ground," mean several things. First, they mean men must acknowledge their link with the earth (whatever sort of world they build), and that the human species is sustained by the same source as the food it raises: "Gourd vine blossom / walls and houses drawn up / from the same soft soil." Furthermore, when the men complete their ritual in the kiva, they reascend to the world of practical affairs ("out there out side all the chores"), but they do so redrawn, as it were, as members of a shared communal and communizing myth. Snyder also notes that the place of the kiva was once "the floor of a sea" back in the prehistoric Permian age. It becomes again a floor, a foundation that perches a society on an earth that has seen vast geologically scaled changes, so vast that the bodies of the men "flap to the limestone blanket." This figure of speech turns the earth into a source of warmth and comfort, but more importantly it sees the normally stable, unyielding land as a flexible, even transitory arrangement. So everything—men, houses, agriculture, animals—is part of a scene of transformed and transforming energies and states of matter that are no more substantial than smoke. Yet the insubstantiality of smoke is controlled and framed, as it were, by the kiva whence it originates, the hole it passes through, and the higher and lower worlds, the passage to which it symbolizes.

Standing at the end of *The Back Country,* this poem becomes more than an anthropological exercise, for we are asked to read it as itself a figure for the back country, which as Snyder has said has three associations, the wilderness, the backward countries, and the back country of the mind with its levels of being in the unconscious. In "Riprap" the stones were models for the density of words, but they were also the bridge to other states and so were also seen as modes of energy. In "Through the Smoke Hole," the kiva symbolizes a place of wholeness but also a process of becoming whole. The kiva is a liminal place of great concentrated imagination, and Snyder knows it is a place of community as well. From this point on, the political vision in Snyder's work derives from increasingly complex mythological figures: the kiva, the tribe, Turtle Island. It is possible to see this angle of vision as a reaction against "the old, dirty countries" whose Buddhist religion Snyder could assimilate but whose social reality offered no practical models. In coming back to America, Snyder gained a sort of abstracting consciousness—which we will see in *Regarding Wave*—that enabled him to reimagine his native country as a mythic Amerindian place, Turtle Island. In the meantime, Snyder did not abandon his trust in physical reality and daily work; he is, if you will, a nonidealizing abstractor.[2]

2. See again Charles Altieri, "Gary Snyder's *Turtle Island*: The Problem of Reconciling the Roles of Seer and Prophet," *Boundary 2,* 6, 3 (Spring 1976): 761–77, where the warning is advanced by Joan Webber, a colleague Altieri cites in a note, that Snyder must borrow the "trappings of a social scientist in order to claim any authority," though in doing so he

The major development in Snyder's vision effected by *The Back Country* is the concern with the unconscious. This is also the most problematic of the three metaphoric meanings of the book's central figure. Using place as a figure for mental energies or conditions is, of course, an ancient metaphoric strategy, and, as Kenneth Burke, among others, has shown, place is built into our language in words and phrases such as "states of mind" and "understanding." Such a strategy also allows Snyder to draw on some of the Freudian insights without committing himself to a full endorsement of the psychoanalytic scheme. The problem comes when we realize Snyder's affinity with such thinkers as R.D. Laing and Norman O. Brown, who tend to equate too readily the conditions of an individual's mental life with the state of the society of which he or she is a member. Here Snyder has links with other poets, such as Robert Bly, who have been criticized for apparently accepting uncritically a reductive equation between individual neurosis and social disorder.[3] For the moment, suffice it to say that Snyder's autobiographical impulse is dominant in *The Back Country,* so whatever political vision the book contains is bound to be drawn in quite personal, individual terms. The argument over how and to what extent individual neurosis mirrors (echoes? contains? symbolizes?—the choice of a verb here will itself demonstrate how problematic the relation is) social disorder will doubtlessly not be easily settled. Of course, the whole question of how to represent the relation, assuming there is one substantial enough to be discussed or analyzed, is, for a poet and his readers, the prior question. Questions of figurative language become central, and this leads us back to the aesthetic economy of the kiva. Because the structure has an individual dimension, since metaphorically the kiva is each member's "head," or mental space, as well as

---

decreases the power of his transforming vision. I would agree, but I see no other ready way, except satire, for any poet to address political problems from a consistent standpoint. However, there is the "new" poetry of Snyder, which I discuss in Chapter 3 below.

3. The forthcoming book by Paul Breslin, *The Poetics of Guilt,* makes the negative case in some detail.

a social dimension, since it is the place where group identity is reaffirmed, Snyder arrives at a satisfying mediation between the two realms of value and experience.

Snyder's work is consonant with the argument in Mary Douglas's *Natural Symbols* (1970), in which she argues that "the body is capable of furnishing a natural system of symbols," but there are "elements in the social system . . . [that tell] how the body should function." Since social groups were themselves often the basis of classificatory thought, the social myths could easily be seen as prior to the individual myths. But such logical priority is not the only determining factor, especially for a poet (and especially for an American poet). Snyder again and again asserts the value of the individual, the locus of desire and the place where balance and order are first experienced. To put it bluntly, there are in Snyder images of perfectly ordered individuals, but there are few perfectly harmonious societies. This overstates the case somewhat, for as we will see shortly, *Earth House Hold* does offer at least a figuration of an achieved social harmony in the metaphor of the tribe. But the experience recorded in *The Back Country* will always have an antinomian cast to it, a sense that personal revitalization does not precede political vision but rather obviates the need for it. To counter that antinomianism we would have to stress the use of the plural in the lines "plain men / come out of the ground." Another way to put this is to see Coyote as only one of the many individuals who use the kiva, so that the celebration of the antisocial can be fully understood only against the backdrop of an ultimately stable political order.

Also, recalling the sense of "Burning the small dead," with its image of "windy fire" as the poetic figure for the various elements of the poem as well as a metaphor for the consciousness that links them, we can see the kiva as an integrating metaphor that could represent the poem itself. Both a meditative and a transformative place, the kiva is both in time and out of time. It can be narrowly conceived and applied, so as to enforce the notion that "history / after the Jurassic is a bore," but it can as well be applied as a figure of all social harmonies. There persists in Snyder's work the ambiguity that binds the meditative, and potentially passive, with the transformative, and potentially activist, understandings of the political realm. In a curious lateral leap, this reminds me of one of the "Hitch Haiku" from "Far West":

> After weeks of watching the roof leak
> > I fixed it tonight
> by moving a single board

This is as perfect as a Zen koan in many ways. The two extreme interpretations would hold that (1) the moving of the single board shows how futile it would have been to patch the entire roof and yet it makes the inconvenience of the weeks-long dripping especially frustrating—both our efforts and our nonefforts often are out of scale; and (2) only by watching the leak for a long period was the economy of repair by a single, simple action possible—watchfulness is the only way to be truly efficient, though it may appear as impotence or stupidity. We might even call the first interpretation the logical one and the second the Zen one. But even this dichotomizing and labeling is part of the Occidental habit of mind; the concealedness of the narrative and its mixture of play and seriousness mark it as Oriental. As a figure for a kind of awareness, or sensibility embedded in gestural awareness (act and knowledge being silent codeterminants), the haiku blends the meditative and the transformative in ways that Snyder has obviously incorporated into the center of his poetics and his politics. As we will see in *Earth House Hold,* a centering figure, in this case the tribe, can resolve and focus normally intractable tensions; whether transformation will consequently be made possible, let alone more likely, as a result of such figuration is a question that lies beyond the figure itself.

Earth House Hold

Though clearly a product of the widespread social and political upheaval of the 1960s, *Earth House Hold* (1969) has several antecedents in American literature. The first comparison that comes to mind is with William Carlos Williams's *In the American Grain* (1925), a book of cultural and political essays that serve to support and enunciate an aesthetic orientation. In both books, moreover, the emphasis is on a countercultural awareness that sets itself against the dominant, hegemonic political forces; for Williams this force is essentially Puritanism, while for Snyder there are industrialism and nationalism. Both books are moral and didactic, yet they never become overtly moralistic; like Pound's *The Spirit of Romance* (1910), they look to persuade by a sweet reasonableness, and whatever larger cultural vision they offer is subsumed in more local, often purely aesthetic questions. But unlike Williams and Pound, Snyder deliberately mixes the modes in *Earth House Hold,* as he presents discursive essays and book reviews alongside extended journal entries, which in turn may include scraps of poetry. The book's subtitle, *Technical Notes and Queries to Fellow Dharma Revolutionaries,* as well as its dedication to Oda Sesso Roshi (1901–1966), Snyder's teacher in the Rinzai sect of which he was a member in the late 1950s and early 1960s, indicates the poet's indebtedness to Eastern philosophy and culture. But it is also possible to see the book as a very American testament—here the prototype would be Thoreau's *Walden*—that mixes personal experience with a universalizing vision addressed to the largest questions. Though Snyder has said that he did not return to America only because his teacher, Oda Sesso, died, we can also see *Earth House Hold* as a post-Buddhist work. The book is in a way his reentry into America, paralleling in that sense the fourth section of *The Back Country,* with its themes of homecoming and reorientation. But the book is also to be read as Snyder's international testament, containing as it does journal entries from the Pacific Northwest, Japan, and the oil tanker Snyder worked on while traveling between the two. Equally, then, the book is post-American and looks forward to the more "philosophical" (using that word in a very restricted way) poetics of *Regarding Wave,* where the emphasis shifts, relatively, from a sense of place to a sense of mind, as the stage where the crucial poetic energies are to be displayed.

But I would suggest yet another model for reading *Earth House Hold*, one that is more intuitive than rational, and suggestive rather than definitive. I think *Earth House Hold* is best read as Snyder's epic—in the sense that epic means a storehouse of cultural ideas and ideals, a compendium of other literary forms, an account of men and gods and how they came to be that way, and an address to the gens, the tribe whose cultural and historical identity the epic seeks to solidify: this is what I have in mind for *Earth House Hold*. What is most clearly *not* epical about the book is its lack of a clear narrative frame. I would explain this by saying that Snyder buries a narrative in the text—the corruption of industrialized society and its redemption by the new revolutionary spirit—but that essentially the political vision of the book mistrusts the usual modes of representation on which traditional narratives rest. Snyder cannot offer himself as hero or as typical man; hence his personal journal entries are especially tentative, exploratory, even self-canceling in parts. Also, the various sects and countercultural groups, which Snyder partially lists as "astronomers, ritualists, alchemists, Albigensians; gnostics and vagantes, right down to Golden Gate Park," merge into a super-identity as the "Great Subculture," and this group has no clear or identifiable narrative. In part, *Earth House Hold* is a book of secrets, secret learning and secret lore, but these secrets do not lie locked up in an esoteric narrative or book of magic symbols. Instead the secrets are everyday, even ordinary, and Snyder defines the bond of identity among the adepts as "a bright and tender look; calmness and gentleness, freshness and ease of manner." The book is a compilation of "technical notes," that is, a gathering of essential information about our relatedness to the environment and our own psyches, individual as well as social, and also "queries," tentative offerings and proposals rather than insistent or programmatic demands. (The book might perhaps be compared to Paul Goodman's *Utopian Essays and Practical Proposals*.)

66

The modern poetic epics that are best known in the English-language tradition, such as Pound's *Cantos* and Williams's *Paterson*, exhibit great difficulty in mediating between the individual speaker and the larger cultural and political audience. Snyder apparently is not comfortable with adopting an epic voice, through the creation of a persona or even through a sort of mythical-literary construct such as Williams's man-speaking-as-a-city in the case of *Paterson*. In this sense, the journal entries are an important part of *Earth House Hold* that not only relates it to such previous books as *Walden* but also stresses the element of personal example and the redemptiveness of daily work that forms the core of Snyder's political vision. Journal entries do not readily yield to literary analysis, and to give the flavor of them would require quoting at great length.[4] The entries are in part logs of daily activity, usually involving a certain amount of physical labor, but they also contain a large amount of observation of the surrounding environment. But equally important are the notations Snyder makes of his readings, as well as his reflections on his ideas, dreams, and fantasies. They have an epic dimension in that they report the language and often the anecdotes of his fellow workers and so serve a sort of folk-art function in preserving parts of the "tale of the tribe." What they avoid doing, I think, is creating any sense of class voyeurism or travel-book color, since they always convey a sense that Snyder was indeed employed at the time and not just visiting or researching the occupations and locales. In this sense they may be among the best writings about work by an American since *Life on the Mississippi*.

Essays form the bulk of *Earth House Hold*, and the most discursive of these present Snyder's political vision in its most direct exposition. Few of Snyder's contemporaries

4. See the remarks on the journals in Sherman Paul, "From Lookout to Ashram: The Way of Gary Snyder," *Iowa Review* 1, 3 (Spring 1970): 76–91, and 1, 4 (Summer 1970): 70–86. Paul posits what strikes me as too linear a development for Snyder, from "social passivity" to "increasing activism and communitarianism," but this essay is a sensitive reading of Snyder's work.

have written in prose, and at such length, of the issues he deals with in such essays as "Buddhism and the Coming Revolution," "Passage to More Than India," "Why Tribe," and "Poetry and the Primitive." Certainly the scale of the thinking in these essays is epical even if the wealth of detail is not. The political thought here can be related to indigenous American traditions, such as Jefferson's pastoral ideals and the antinomian attack on repressive institutions that makes up much of Emersonian transcendentalism. But the essays contain an essentially utopian vision rather than a partisan or practical one, and so they are best read in that context instead of as social commentary or political analysis. Even the constant references to decay and the uselessness of current Western political values do not have the polemical tone or texture one might suspect from their content. Nor, on the other hand, does one get a sense of wooly-headedness; again, this flavor is reinforced by the journal entries, which give the whole book an air of thoughtfulness and urgent resolve. Yet there is something at the same time tentative—some would call it poetic—about the writing here, in these "notes" and "queries," a reluctance to resort to definitions or axioms that might make the arguments rigid. In strictly literary terms, this mixture of tones comes as a genuine accomplishment, and I think it is an important part of Snyder's political vision as well, which relies crucially on a mixture of meditativeness and energy. Here is a passage from "Buddhism and the Coming Revolution":

> The mercy of the West has been social revolution; the mercy of the East has been individual insight into the basic self/void. We need both. They are both contained in the traditional three aspects of the Dharma path: wisdom (prajña), meditation (dhyāna), and morality (śila). Wisdom is intuitive knowledge of the mind of love and clarity that lies beneath one's ego-driven anxieties and aggressions. Meditation is going into the mind to see this for yourself—over and over again, until it becomes the mind you live in. Morality is bringing it back out in the way you live, through personal example and responsible action, ultimately toward the true community (sangha) of "all beings." This last aspect means,

for me, supporting any cultural and economic revolution that moves clearly toward a free, international, classless world. It means using such means as civil disobedience, outspoken criticism, protest, pacifism, voluntary poverty and even gentle violence if it comes to a matter of restraining some impetuous redneck. It means affirming the widest possible spectrum of non-harmful individual behavior—defending the right of individuals to smoke hemp, eat peyote, be polygynous, polyandrous or homosexual. Worlds of behavior and custom long banned by the Judaeo-Capitalist-Christian-Marxist West. It means respecting intelligence and learning, but not as greed or means to personal power. Working on one's own responsibility, but willing to work with a group. "Forming the new society within the shell of the old"—the I.W.W. slogan of fifty years ago.

The vision of a "free, international, classless" world evolves out of a distinctive array of utopian elements, and the controlling figure of the "Dharma path" contains three values—wisdom, meditation, and morality—that clearly have application in Western as well as Eastern philosophy. Given the sort of cultural cross-fertilization that took place between Thoreau and Gandhi, and Gandhi and Martin Luther King, Snyder's transcultural vocabulary should come as no surprise. But we should notice that the vision sets itself against (or perhaps above) both East and West, while at the same time recycling the particularities that range from "sangha" to the IWW. This ability, or at least willingness, on Snyder's part to enunciate the largest scale for his vision while shoring it up with particular notions and experiences stands as one of the most distinctive features of his style.

All in all, *Earth House Hold* is a remarkable book not only in its own terms but also because it was written by a postwar American poet. The structure of its political ideas can stand up to critical scrutiny, and in fact deserves such scrutiny, as I hope to show presently. But again I stress the unique syncretic quality of Snyder's vision, and again I cannot resist calling it quintessentially American in its relation to its own sources. Much of Snyder's utopianism has clear European roots, yet it tries to draw up the terms of its discourse in a worldwide context. This very gesture, at once a refusal, a longing, and a resolute plainspokenness, places Snyder in a tradition of American political idealism. Yet this idealism thrives in a context of physical reality; it is *almost* as if Snyder's main political lessons are built solely on how he worked—as a logger, lookout, or sailor—in a demanding physical labor whose very praxis contained all the negative and positive wisdom he could ever lay claim to. But those labors, those physical conditions, always take place against the American dream of an original innocence, a primal clarity that is envisioned as a redeemed temporal order and that is one of the essential elements in the utopian imagination. This other realm has a wisdom of its own to offer, as it both preserves and enables physical labor.

Snyder's political vision amalgamates ideas and values from a number of different cultures, and so is not easily susceptible to a reductive or structuralist analysis. It is possible to argue that for Snyder the main element in his vision is a syncretizing process, a way of insuring maximum adaptability with maximum diversity. In this, his vision is analogous with his view of nature and the striving for ecological wholeness and complexity. Still, the originality of Snyder's amalgam rests on a set of utopian ideas that were developed and transmitted historically. As such, these ideas have been put to other uses and have been studied in a variety of ways. One particularly well-known study is Karl Mannheim's *Ideology and Utopia*.[5] In this book Mannheim defines four utopian ideals, locating them in a historical scheme that is centered on European social and political thought since the middle ages. Mannheim's book was written before the specter of ethnocentrism had been raised by scholars, and the historical scheme is not nearly as rigorous as that of many subsequent works. Also, Mannheim's typology assumes something vaguely like an idealized, absolute status. Since Mannheim borrows from Max Weber's ideal types, he is

5. I use the paperback edition published as a Harvest book by Harcourt Brace Jovanovich. The book first appeared in German in 1929.

able to avoid the problem of establishing whether his categories have a secure metaphysical basis. The four types of utopian thinking, therefore, are not explicitly labeled as eternal forms, and in fact they are often shown modifying one another in the heated struggles of historical reality, and existing as the expression of certain material situations. Suffice it to say that I offer Mannheim's types as a way of seeing the extent of Snyder's syncretism, and I imply no more absolute value for them than Mannheim claims. Furthermore, I mention their limitations with an awareness that the types are nevertheless formulated by a scholar with a vast range of learning.

Since my interest in Mannheim's types is heuristic and purposive, I will resort to brute summary by offering a table of features for the four types. I do this knowing that Mannheim himself probably would not approve and realizing that many of his subtler points will be lost. Again, I plead expediency, since I want to focus on the chiliastic type but also to modify it in terms of Snyder's vision. Mannheim identifies as the main characteristic of each view what he calls its time-sense; this includes an understanding both of how history is oriented toward a goal and of how such orientation determines the feel of ordinary, everyday existence. In addition to the time-sense Mannheim discusses the various types in terms of how social forces are focused (whether through individual actions or collective or institutional forms) and how each type conceives of the human ability to know and control the shape of events. He also posits a conception of how the commonweal is to measure or express its success, in material or spiritual terms. Obviously the following table obscures key points; for example, the conservative utopia is the one most willing to accept the social conditions as given and so tends to have "no predisposition towards theorizing." Its base of wealth is often material, though it offers, whenever it does theorize, certain spiritual values, such as order and tradition, as justification for its actions. Another example, one that will concern Snyder's vision, is the chiliastic sense of revolutionary anarchism, which is seen as affecting everyone, and is hence collective, but whose fervor and hope are often kindled and transmitted by individual, charismatic leaders. But here is the table:

Type	Temporal Order/Goal	Agency of Social Force	Nature of Will	Base of Wealth
Chiliastic	Erratic/ Transcendent	Collective	Free	Spiritual
Liberal	Progressive/ Remote	Individual	Free	Spiritual
Conservative	Fixed/Nostalgic	Individual	Determinate	Spiritual
Socialist- Communist	Developmental/ Remote	Collective	Controlled	Material

Snyder's vision is largely socialist, but it includes many features that derive from the chiliastic type, especially as it tends toward revolutionary anarchism. By using nature and his ecstatic insights into its power and order, Snyder clearly evokes the chiliastic emphasis on "absolute presentness." As Mannheim describes it, "the present becomes the breach through which what was previously inward bursts out suddenly, takes hold of the outer world and transforms it." We can see this irruption of consciousness in *Myths & Texts,* in section 8 of "Burning," for example, as well as in Snyder's insistence on the value of the "power-vision in solitude." Chiliastic feelings are also lodged in Snyder's urge to move onward from Marxist politics and to posit a model that is both transcendent and yet rooted in the physical world, namely the "vast interrelated network in which all objects and creatures are necessary and illuminated," as he puts it in *Earth House Hold.*

Perhaps the most important chiliastic element in Snyder's thought is his willingness to use a variety of metaphors or master terms for centering political values. Mannheim argues that the "essential feature of Chiliasm is its tendency always to dissociate itself from its own images and symbols." This tendency derives from the anarchist's sense that proposing a single term, or set of terms, to govern political imagination and action will inevitably result in some oppressive institutionalization. But again, to resort to a political truism, there can be no government without some authority structure. Snyder does not enunciate a strict anarchist position, and he seems willing to accept some authority structures such as the tribe and a version of the extended (nonnuclear) family. This leads to that crucial distinction between the temporal senses in chiliasm and those in socialism. For the socialist, the temporal sense is developmental, that is, it borrows from the liberal the idea of linear progress. This linearity, however, is importantly modified to express a sense of controllable development. For the natural progress of the Enlightenment liberal, the socialist substitutes a belief in what Mannheim calls a "coherent, critical method," one that aims to demonstrate how the present state of society contains both the sedimented mistaken ideas of the past as well as the progressive possibilities of dynamic, nonabstract forces that work toward freedom and justice. The liberal utopian tends to replace revolutionary fervor with rational trust; the socialist sees ideas as expressive results of determinate situations, and so ideas can serve as guides, positive and negative, to identifying the proper liberating forces at work (or buried) in society. Snyder draws on this socialist tradition of critical thought, for example, when he sees that Buddhism did not prevent the Chinese from overexploiting their forests. Socialism maintains an uneasy balance between its own utopian and scientific impulses, of course, and this balance, with all its uneasiness, affects Snyder as well. Though his aversion to any sort of Leninist model of a controlling vanguard party is obvious, Snyder has not really set out how the socialist utopia is to be achieved in terms of political actions that address the mass, urbanized existence of industrial society.

Here is where his mixture of chiliastic and socialist ideas comes into sharp relief. Snyder uses the idea of the tribe in ways that suggest an emergent, self-conscious, critical revolutionary awareness that coalesces in a self-identifying group. Yet such a group identity ought not to be based on, or lead to, the kind of authority structure epitomized by the modern state. This means there can be no hierarchy or specialization. Furthermore, the new group must be composed of individuals who have exorcised the forces that would give leaders "a hook into the social psyche," as Snyder puts it in "Why Tribe," another key essay from *Earth House Hold.* Here Snyder argues for a revolutionary scheme containing both chiliastic and socialist elements. The members of the tribe clearly have a level of awareness superior to that of most people, for they have achieved a measure of liberation from the false values of civilization. What comes next, however, is presented as a "new step," implying that a controlled, developmental revolution, such as a socialist would approve, is now possible, even imminent. Yet at the same time Snyder argues that as far as the revolution is concerned, "people are trying it out right now"; here we see the chiliastic impulse to assert the notion of "absolute presentness." And in Snyder's use of present-day examples—"the signal is a bright and tender look"—we can see the tendency of the chiliast to point to and yet beyond actual cases.

Here is the relevant passage:

> Consequently the modern Tribesman . . . is the most relevant type in contemporary society. Nationalism, warfare, heavy industry and consumership, are already out dated and useless. The next great step of mankind is to step into the nature of his own mind—the real question is "just what is consciousness?"—And we must make the most intelligent and creative use of science in exploring these questions. The man of wide international experience, much learning and leisure—luxurious product of our long and sophisticated history—may with good reason wish to live simply, with few tools and minimal clothes, close to nature.

Nearly every sentence here calls out for a gloss, some negative, some positive. Start with the description of the Tribesman as "most relevant." This clearly derives from Snyder's axiology, for what relevant means is "most valuable," yet it avoids saying "most dominant" or "most authoritative." Likewise, any sharp choice between the Tribesman deriving his or her identity individually or from a group is bracketed, as it were, and we get something like an Emersonian majority of one. Later Snyder actually gives the supposed number of tribesmen as 1 million in America, another million in England and Europe, and a "vast underground in Russia." (Curiously, he does not mention Asia or Africa.) Then the claim that the ills of modern society are "already out dated and useless" has a definite chiliastic ring to it. So far the tone of the argument is definitely anarchistic, but then we are told "we *must* make . . . use of science" (my italics) to achieve the next step. Here the socialist sense of developmental time asserts itself, and an almost liberal notion of rational progress appears as well. The last sentence returns to a chiliastic scheme as it envisions a total reversal of values in the psyche of the individual.

This is also a good place to draw attention to the context of multinational capitalism. Snyder sees "the man of wide international experience" as the product of a "long and sophisticated history." Implicit in this is the idea that nationalism, and the existence of the nation-state, is a historical stage that has made possible the modern industrialized world, but now this stage is "useless" and even obstructive of progress. Yet a further implicit meaning seems to be that only those people who have such wide international experience will be able to free themselves from the fetters of nationalism and the complex hungers of industrialized society. From the capitalist point of view, the next step, of course, is multinational capitalism, with its enormous network of tourist-related industries, runaway shops using cheap peasant labor, the manipulation of peripheral, so-called third-world economies, chiefly by encumbering them with massive debts, and the support system of nation-state rivalries that can be used to implement the policies of the superpowers. Snyder's vision of the next step radically opposes that of the managers of the new mulitnational order, yet the vision is itself a product of historical and social forces. The chiliasm that longs for an instant conversion to humility and ecstasy clashes with a socialism, part utopian, part scientific, that realizes all processes, human and natural, are possible only within boundaries and according to laws that govern the availability and conversion of energy and raw material. This volatile mixture of rational and irrational elements can be understood as both the unwitting product and the unavailing counterbalance of the cultural genocide that comes in the wake of multinational capitalism. On the one hand, our awareness of the primitive is made possible by capitalist expansion brought on by an ever increasing need for raw material, yet our science knows enough to see that unlimited exploitation will ultimately destroy otherwise renewable resources. Thus the primitive comes to us as the endangered; it is understood, in other words, in the context of the conflict between *our* needs and *our* long-term awareness (some would say conscience). But within *our* context, nevertheless. For Snyder, primitive man and his values present us with an object lesson in the fragility of environments. But primitive societies cannot in themselves offer a solution on how to deindustrialize modern society, since they have no direct experience of industrial capitalism. Nor can they offer a way to the next step in consciousness, since they do not have the "long and sophisticated history" that has led to the current step. Somehow the irrational "absolute presentness" we associate with primitive man will have to be reinserted into that long torturous development toward higher consciousness that can be mapped only by rational understanding. There can be no higher sophistication, Snyder argues, without a reprimitivizing of our lives. Meanwhile, the multinational capitalist system will continue to manipulate our most primitive needs and fears—the hooks in our social psyche—in order to adjust ever more sophisticated social controls. The lines that separate the erection of the primitive as a value for harmonizing social and political consciousness from the utilization of the primitive as yet another marketable commodity become harder and harder to etch clearly. *Earth House Hold*, and Snyder's political vision in general, is poised on a point of difficult balance, since it shares with many other critical visions the difficult task of addressing a social order that is adroit at absorbing all opposing views.

This is also another version of the questions posed near the beginning of this chapter, for we have to ask if such a figure as the Tribesman can best serve as a depiction of current social conditions, as a putative solution to those conditions, or as a criticism, highly subjectivized, that ultimately stands helpless before them? We are asking, in other words, what is the status of Snyder's metaphors? Can they themselves become master terms in a new social and political order, and if not, does this inability invalidate them?[6] These questions become even more urgent with Snyder's next book, *Regarding Wave*, in which the implicit claims for the metaphoric center become more demanding.

Regarding Wave

As a way of opening the discussion of *Regarding Wave*, I would like to suggest some approaches to Snyder's use of Buddhist thought and culture in the overall shape of his vision. There are at least two obvious points here: first, Snyder's knowledge of Buddhism seems deep and his appreciation of its cultural values appears genuine, if not crucial, in his growth as a poet; second, only an expert in Buddhism (which I am not) could make a final assessment of the accuracy or propriety of Snyder's transcultural borrowings. As far as the second point goes, in a way all such borrowings are by definition inaccurate or improper, since they appropriate parts of a whole according to needs or principles not necessarily consonant with the whole. Yet Snyder argues that his insights into Buddhism taught him about the interrelatedness of all things, and this key notion harmonized with the wisdom he had derived from his study of the American Indian. But if such transcultural

6. The material on this subject is extensive, but two works I have consulted are George Lakoff and Mark Johnson, *Metaphors We Live By* (Chicago:University of Chicago Press, 1980) and *The Social Use of Metaphor,* ed. J. David Sapir and J. Christopher Crocker (Philadelphia: University of Pennsylvania Press, 1977). A very useful overview and analysis is Paul Ricoeur, *The Rule of Metaphor* (Toronto: University of Toronto Press, 1977).

fertilization provided only a reinforcement for existing predilections, it would hardly be worth pursuing. Instead, such empathizing with and reimagining of cultural visions often provide poets with figurative resolutions or clarifications of their personal angles of vision. Speaking very generally, I would suggest that the emphasis on the pragmatic and local awareness of the environment that Snyder derived from Amerindian culture was supplemented by his Buddhist awareness of an ascetic and even mystical approach to the cosmos and the individual mind. Obviously Amerindian myth has a cosmic component and Buddhism formulates values that work on an everyday, practical level. But Snyder came to Buddhist philosophy after a thorough grounding in both the personal experience and the academic study of Amerindian culture. By sharing in the interest in Eastern religions, Snyder was like many writers of the postwar era, especially those on the West Coast, though his involvement was clearly part of a lifelong, temperamentally grounded study of vision itself. For Snyder, Buddhism was a completion as much as an initiation.

Snyder was for several years a practicing Buddhist monk, sitting in meditation and living in the ascetic discipline of the monastery. In some way the monastery doubtlessly served him as an image of community, a more restricted model of the idea of tribe that he later developed. Also, the asceticism of the monastery obviously answered to Snyder's interest in an "objectivist" poetic. But the larger ramifications of these needs for a sense of community and for a style of language use and personal habit are harder to trace and to connect to Buddhist thought. One could, for example, read much of Snyder's work and not be aware of how elite the Rinzai Zen sect of Buddhism is in its separation between monks and laity.[7] In most of Zen the only spiritual value the layman can obtain is through giving alms to the monks. The sense of community is purchased, then, by a very strong exclusionary

7. One corrective passage is the second paragraph of the key essay "Buddhism and the Coming Revolution," from *Earth House Hold*.

practice. Much of Zen's popularity in this country, among artists and bohemian groups, was the result of popularizers such as D.T. Suzuki and Alan Watts, who did not stress such aspects of Buddhism's asceticism and elitism. As for the question of language use and personal habit, Zen's stress on silence and the ineffability of the "way" clearly connects with the tight-lipped, understated ethos of the American West. But further back in the history of Buddhism there is a tangle of sects and reform movements whose main objective is a purification and safeguarding of texts, messages, and rituals in an attempt to ward off secularization and vulgarization. Again, many rigorous elements of Zen tend to be lost in the transcultural appropriation, though Snyder himself was in no way lax or indulgent in addressing these aspects of a tightly woven cultural vision.

Chief among the elements of Buddhism that influenced Snyder was the teaching of the Rinzai sect, especially as reflected in the *Recorded Sayings of Ch'an Master Lin-chi*, [8] a portion of which Snyder helped translate. Rinzai (d. 866) was a Chinese Buddhist and so was aware of the roots of the concept of *dharma* in the Way of Taoism. There are, according to one Western scholar,[9] three main Rinzai teachings: (1) the secular and the sacred are not to be distinguished, (2) one must be master of every situation and the place where you stand is the true place, and (3) mind is without form and follows the ten directions, that is, the senses and bodily movements. Snyder's poetry draws on all of these teachings, and *Regarding Wave* is especially dependent on the third. There was also a fourteenth-century Rinzai adherent, Ikkyu, who formulated teachings that influenced the work in this particular volume. Ikkyu said that sutras, the Buddhist form of sacred aphorism, are recorded by wind or rain or inscribed in the patterning of snowdrifts. Equally important for Snyder is the poem by Ikkyu that celebrates the incident in which Rinzai burned

8. Translated by Ruth Fuller Sasaki (Kyoto: Institute for Zen Studies, 1975). See p. xii for the acknowledgment to Snyder for his completion of the unfinished fourth draft in spring 1968.

9. Jon Carter Covell, *Unravelling Zen's Red Thread* (Elizabeth, N.J.:Hollym International, 1980), pp. 57–64.

his desk and records at the end of his life; this was understood as an emblem of the holocaust at the end of time. A poem in *Regarding Wave*, "To Fire," has one of its antecedents in Ikkyu's poem. But such source-hunting, though useful and even necessary for a precise sense of Snyder's command and use of his material, is best reserved for a more local study. I would like to suggest some of the broader contexts in which Snyder adapts Buddhist values.

According to Jon Carter Covell, Hinayana Buddhism tries to deny the passions, and Mahayana tries to sublimate them into enlightenment, but Zen Buddhism says that the passions *are* enlightenment. In its spiritual strategy, Zen employs a large portion of mystical contemplation, as exemplified in its use of the koan, or riddle. This acceptance of the passions and emphasis on contemplation began to dominate Snyder's poetry in the late 1960s, especially as it developed between *The Back Country* and *Regarding Wave*. We can speculate that after the daily discipline of the monastery, which Snyder experienced off and on in the early 1960s, he decided that any attempt to rationalize and ritualize spiritual belief was unproductive. Instead he would emphasize the positive, celebratory aspects of Buddhism, as presented in Zen and Tantric teachings. Furthermore, while not abandoning his appreciation of an ascetic use of language, he would allow himself more play, more riddlesome dancing among the tacit or connotative levels of words and utterances. This produced the poems of *Regarding Wave*, especially those in the first two sections, which utilize a more evocative, richly metaphoric approach (where the poems of the *Riprap* period tended to be precise and metonymic).

To abstract yet further, we can borrow from Max Weber two contrastive models of religious ritual.[10] First, there is the ritual that is based on the value of single actions. In this framework an accounting is taken of every action, and its practitioners generally eschew the "yearning for rebirth in the strict sense of an ethic of inwardness." The

10. In his *The Sociology of Religion* (Boston: Beacon Press, 1963), chap. 10, "The Different Roads to Salvation."

other sense of ritual views actions as symptomatic of an "underlying ethical total personality." This sort of ritual stresses the ethics of inwardness. Snyder's adaptation of Zen principles clearly aligns him with the second type of ritual. In this adaptation, Snyder's idealist emphasis on mental states receives great stress, as the closing lines of the first poem in *Regarding Wave* make clear:

Ah, trembling spreading radiating wyf
racing zebra
catch me and fling me wide
To the dancing grain of things
of my mind!

The "wyf" here is the Anglo-Saxon word that serves as the root of both wave and wife and also stands as the metaphoric radius from which all the images of the poem arise and pulse. The "dancing grain of things" is Snyder's formulation for the orderliness of natural processes, recalling the flux of his early poetics with its emphasis on change and transformation as well as on the harmony of objects. The last phrase of the poem ambiguously merges the noumenal and phenomenal realms, uniting world and mind, as the movement of the passage joins the experience of ego-loss ("fling me wide") with personal ecstasy.

The seeking of patterns in nature, the chief preoccupation of *Regarding Wave,* serves as Snyder's way of figuratively representing the values of the religious ritual that rely on an underlying totality. But the paratactic proliferation of metaphor—wife, wave, racing zebra, and so forth—is a way of rationalizing the spiritual realm by domesticating and naturalizing it rather than relying on ecstatic or intense moments. All of this in turn borrows from the Zen habits of contemplating the ineffable, manifesting spiritual truth in equivalences, and always pointing beyond definition or equation—while yet using it—toward a silent, inward comprehension. Snyder's use of Buddhism plays a key role in his understanding of ritual, for it allows him to be positive about patterns and a supportive stability without becoming static and stale in his religious watchfulness.

This flexibility at the level of ritual, or more accurately at the level of ritualized awareness, is consonant with another important element in Buddhism that influenced Snyder's poetry and vision: the sense of a sacred tradition that extends in historical time but avoids strict adherence to a single master text. Buddhism as a whole, but Zen in a special way, transmits its values through personal instruction and discipleship. Snyder shows his appreciation of this practice in the essay from *Earth House Hold* titled "Record of the Life of the Ch'an Master Po-Chang Huai-Hai," a teacher who preceded Rinzai (Lin-Chi) by two generations. Again, the practice of referring to the lives of the masters stresses the importance of the underlying personality, since the master must utilize personal example and the life-embodiment of values in training students. No concretized or rationalized method of instruction or behavior can replace the emphasis on personal commitment and inner development so valued in Buddhism. This aspect of the religion reinforces as well the predilection to play with metaphors, freely substituting an array of figures rather than limiting the interpreter to certain highly sanctioned images imbedded in a single master text, as tends to be the case in the Judeo-Christian tradition. As some semioticians have suggested, cultures can be divided into two distinct types, based on how they generate their sign systems. Some cultures stress the sense of normative texts, whereas others "model themselves as a system of rules that determine the creation of texts."[11] The former orientation, of which Judeo-Christianity would be an example, leads to a value system based on correct and incorrect acts or beliefs. Buddhism, exemplifying the latter sort of sign system, develops its values around a distinction between organized and nonorganized behavior. Snyder's personal ethos is much closer to the Buddhist tradition in this regard.

One of the sections of *Regarding Wave* includes a group of five poems that exemplify a use of paratactic metaphors

11. Yu. M. Lotman and B. A. Uspensky, "On the Semiotic Mechanism of Culture," *New Literary History* 9, 2 (Winter 1978): 218. The argument is much more complex than the use to which I put it here.

in which a field of several figures is defined through a series of interconnected equivalences. In each poem the title gives a sort of focal point for the metaphoric series, but even here the emphasis is on process, on rules, rather than on objects or fixed hierarchical relations. Here is one of the poems, called "Song of the Taste":

Eating the living germs of grasses
Eating the ova of large birds

  the fleshy sweetness packed
  around the sperm of swaying trees

The muscles of the flanks and thighs of
    soft-voiced cows
  the bounce in the lamb's leap
  the swish in the ox's tail

Eating roots grown swoll
    inside the soil

Drawing on life of living
  clustered points of light spun
    out of space
hidden in the grape.

Eating each other's seed
    eating
ah, each other.

Kissing the lover in the mouth of bread:
    lip to lip.

The poem clearly draws on the traditional equation between seeds as a symbol of natural growth, seeds as emblems of sexual union, and seeds as conveyors of spiritual and mental life. Just as traditional, perhaps, is the stress on process and flux that results from the use of participles. But what is striking about the poem is how the relative status of each dimension—animals, tubers, fruit, human procreative fluids—does not resolve into a hierarchy of realms where one aspect or relationship is used only to illustrate some more correct understanding. The poem is less normative than organized, and it is organized around a series of equal awarenesses. Even the last images can be read as very erotic, as a picture of oral-genital sexual union, or as almost genteel, as a polite and ordinary kiss on the mouth. The poem is about taste in a strictly gustatory sense, but it is also about decorum in a cultural sense, for it equates an emblem of civility with an emblem of appetite.

These suggestions about Snyder's use of Buddhist culture may also illumine the political awareness in *Regarding Wave*. Much of this volume is dominated by the spirit of a poem such as "Song of the Taste," and though specific American and Oriental places are named and celebrated in the book, the poetry searches for abstract patterns more than detailed images. Often the patterns can be daring in their inventiveness, as in "It," where the coming together of two meteorological fronts in a typhoon is equated with reading Blake's poetry:

> mind-fronts meeting
> bite back at each other
> whirl up a Mother Tongue.

There is also a group of poems that celebrate Snyder's marriage and the birth of his child ("Burning Island," "The Bed in the Sky," "Kai, Today," and several others); these poems reach back thematically to the celebration of family stability in the Japan poems from *Riprap*. But in the two final sections of *Regarding Wave*, "Long Hair" and "Target Practice," Snyder turns to more overtly political subjects. "Target Practice" is composed chiefly of brief poems, some haiku-like, others more suggestive of koans. The last section of the final poem, "Civilization," reads like this:

> When creeks are full
> The poems flow
> When creeks are down
> We heap stones

The interrelatedness of work and culture is represented by the common image of a riverbed, though one realm of activity suggests the stones and the other the water. "Flow" and "heap" are complementary processes, not ranked in values but alternating as part of a larger unified activity made necessary according to the needs of the community. Poetry and the real work are both seen as ways of nourishing the community and integrating its needs into the environmental limits and riches.

The community and its needs serve as the subject of many of the poems in "Long Hair." The first of these poems is one of Snyder's most explicit political statements, and it enunciates almost all of the themes we have been tracking in his work thus far. It begins with an image of space, but it also uses space as metaphor for forms of awareness and the placing of values. The poem then goes on to play with a metaphor, turning a political term, communism, into a figure of human and natural integration, Communionism. This allows Snyder to echo the image of ingestion and nourishment that informs not only "Song of the Taste" but many other poems in *Regarding Wave*. This body-centered political ethic is responded to dialectically in the second half of the poem, where Snyder builds a series of subjunctive syllogisms into a plea for the importance of mind-altering ritual. The ritual, in this case the chanted Buddhist formula of the mantra, unites the images of mouth, seed, and speech. Here is the complete poem, called "Revolution in the Revolution in the Revolution":

> The country surrounds the city
> The back country surrounds the country
>
> "From the masses to the masses" the most
> Revolutionary consciousness is to be found
> Among the most ruthlessly exploited classes:
> Animals, trees, water, air, grasses
>
> We must pass through the stage of the
> "Dictatorship of the Unconscious" before we can
> Hope for the withering-away of the states
> And finally arrive at true Communionism.

> If the capitalists and imperialists
>   are the exploiters, the masses are the workers.

> and the party
> is the communist.

If civilization
> is the exploiter, the masses is nature.
> > and the party
> > is the poets.

If the abstract rational intellect
> is the exploiter, the masses is the unconscious.
> > and the party
> > is the yogins.

& POWER
comes out of the seed-syllables of mantras.

The title of the poem can be read as a witty amalgam of Trotskyist theories of "permanent revolution" and Gertrude Stein's play on ontological identity in her statement about "a rose." But though the poem does decidedly have its share of wit and play, it also clearly announces Snyder's political beliefs in a straightforward way. Many modernists might be dismayed at its refusal to dramatize rather than state its argument, and some Marxists would bemoan its revisionist muddling with the nonhuman realm. However, the poem can best be read as a testament to Snyder's unique synthesis, what we might almost call his Buddhist Marxism.

The phrase that begins the second stanza may be read as a key to the poem, for it offers at least two meanings. First, it can refer to the masses of the nonhuman world (animals, trees, and so on) serving the human masses, or conversely the humans tending (and tending to) the realms of the nonhuman. Secondly, the phrase carries a suggestion of transmission, a handing on or over to one party of the dialectic the principles and values of the other party. The "from . . . to" construction connotes transformation, tradition, metamorphosis (as the "stage" image of the third stanza suggests), struggle, and even revelation. The use of words like *hope* and *true* in the third stanza, as well as the coinage of *Communionism*, which nicely translates Snyder's other terms of *interbirth* and *relatedness*, unabashedly declares the religious ground of the poet's political vision.

The poem also playfully substitutes *Unconscious* for *proletariat,* and so turns toward a mental rather than a social or class basis for its mediating figure. The second part of the poem further explores this substitution, again proceeding playfully by a series of would-be syllogisms to a Buddhist conclusion: revolution is made by organized shapely behavior. The Buddhist eightfold way (right conduct, right speech, and so on) is encapsulated in the "seed-syllables" that produce "POWER" by harmonizing with the wavelike structure of both the universe and the disciplined consciousness: "the dancing grain of things / of my mind!"

Snyder speaks in *Earth House Hold* of long hair as a symbol of the acceptance of appetite and change, a willingness to "go *through* the powers of nature." This "way" is the opposite of the way of the ascetic and leads to a celebration of the primitive in human nature. The Dictatorship of the Unconscious will be recognized not as the mere anarchy that Yeats dreaded but as the uncovering of that totally integrated personality that is otherwise rationalized and fragmented by the social order of industrial capitalism. Such dictatorship also is an embrace of energy rather than a suppression of it, and it acknowledges "the marvelous emptiness in all possibilities and directions." Like Freud's, Snyder's unconscious is amoral, or premoral, and the laws of identity and contrariety do not apply to it. This is Snyder's reinterpretation of the Buddhist void, a concept he has wrestled with since the third section of *Myths & Texts.* (The essay "Dharma Queries," in *Earth House Hold,* shows Snyder at his most speculative, his most cosmological, but it is also a good place to see the underpinning of his political vision.) The party that will guide the transformation and liberation is differently identified at each level of revolutionary activity, but communists, poets, and yogis are, if we read the poem's title in yet another way, revolutionized versions of each other. As the poet completes the revolution of the communist by bringing culture, music, and dance into the order of social and economic justice, so the yogi revolutionizes poetry by providing it with that final cosmic consciousness in which the "jewelled net" of all interrelated things is perceived and revered. The real work, organized and humanized by utopian communism, and poetry, the harmonizing of cultural understanding, are brought together and fully realized by the breath that unites the pulse of the individual and the recurrent growth of the universe. Again, as with the paratactic metaphors of "Song of the Taste," each revolution regulates and requires the other.

In a few poems in the "Long Hair" section, Snyder's vision is not always optimistic. For example, just before the poem called "The Fire," Snyder offers a bleak vision of commodity fetishism in "The Trade," a dream-vision poem with a definite nightmarish cast.

> The things of people of that century, in their style,
>   clinging garb made on machines,
>
> Were trading all their precious time
>   for things

"That century" is identified as the twentieth, and the formulation that opens the poem—"I found myself inside a massive concrete shell"—could be a dream-vision or could be read literally. The phrase "in their style" might even contain a condescension not usually found in Snyder. But the juxtaposition of this poem with "Fire" strongly implies that the asceticism and withdrawal that are always present and sometimes dominant in Snyder's vision can be as animating as his revolutionary hope. In another poem, "In the Night, Friend," Snyder records the political suspicion and hatred that accompany social upheaval. But by and large, the poet does not turn to the politics of ressentiment except to record its presence and to note how it distorts the harmonized vision that is both the true cause and the desired effect of revolution.[12]

12. The plotting of history and historical narrative in a literary or rhetorical form is the subject of Hayden White's *Metahistory* (Baltimore: The Johns Hopkins University Press, 1973). Snyder and Allen Ginsberg have both equivocated about the end of the story in regard to industrial capitalism, though Snyder has maintained a more comic view and Ginsberg has lately drifted into a tragic one. But Snyder's comic view is

Buddhism serves Snyder not only as a source of metaphor but also as a source of an attitude toward metaphor. As with the chiliastic imagination, Snyder's Buddhism offers its figurations as a series of equally supportive and clarifying gestures. In a loose sense, if one is to take seriously the Buddhist metaphor of reality as a jeweled net in which "the universe and all its creatures" are seen as "acting in natural response and mutual interdependence," then no metaphor is possible, since all is contained in all to begin with. More precisely, in such a view metaphor will not have the transgressive or daring quality it has in, say, modernist or surrealist writing. Metaphor will be healing and corrective rather than normative, disruptive, or innovative. This is the most positive way to construe Snyder's transcultural borrowings, which can be seen as made necessary by, and leading to, a universalist vision in which cultural specificity is caught up, preserved, and yet altered into a vision that is essentially religious. It is in *Regarding Wave* that this universalist cast to Snyder's thought first received full expression. Generally speaking, in this book Snyder used a full, or if you will looser, sense of figuration so that the specter of cultural monism and sterility that is portended in multinational capitalism is driven off by the utopian merging of the fundamental affirmations of Eastern and Western philosophy into a vision of healing power. What remained for Snyder to do, and this is the task of *Turtle Island* (1974), was to reimagine a specific place and culture with and in the terms of a universalizing myth. The real work in this regard is to locate utopia and to consecrate everyday labor without resort to a merely metaphorical gesture.

---

essentially pastoral, and Ginsberg's tragic sense takes on a threnodic cast, rather than, say a satiric one. An analogy with two well-known movies, both of which base their vision on a total rejection of capitalist values, might be relevant. In Godard's *Weekend* one of the characters says that the only way to overcome the horror of the bourgeoisie is with still more horror. Alain Tanner's *Jonah Will Be 25 in the Year 2000* features a history teacher who speaks of the folds in history and the openings that are interconnected by the superimposition such folds make possible. He says the holes in time through which the prophets see the future are the same holes the historian must use to see the past. Godard shows individualism at the end of its tether, replete with images of forced linearity; Tanner begins to reimagine community, even in the act of historicizing, as present in folds and openings.

III. Mediations

> The poetic imagination . . . is apt to get claustrophobia when it is allowed to talk only about human nature and sub-human nature; and poets are happier as servants of religion than of politics, because the transcendental and apocalyptic perspectives of religion come as a tremendous emancipation of the imaginative mind.
>
> —Northrop Frye

There is a lovely, goofy moment in Jack Kerouac's *The Dharma Bums*. Japhy Ryder, Kerouac's fictional portrait of Snyder, and Ray Smith, Kerouac's narrator and self-portrait, have been mountain climbing. Japhy epitomizes the dedication of the unending religious search by recalling the Zen saying, "When you get to the top of the mountain, keep climbing." Ray is also a "religious searcher" but much less adept at outdoor skills than Japhy, much less self-assured in general. At the start of chapter 12, "suddenly everything was just like jazz: it happened in one insane second or so: I looked up and saw Japhy *running down the mountain* in huge twenty-foot leaps." Ray has a conversion of sorts: "in that flash I realized *it's impossible to fall off mountains you fool* and with a yodel of my own I suddenly got up and began running down the mountain after him." The guru and the disciple arrive below, and, with Japhy "already taking his shoes off and pouring sand and pebbles out," Ray is able to confirm the importance of the lessons that exist outside the text, the truths that only the individual incident and the individual consciousness can embody. "It was great. I took off my sneakers and poured out a couple of buckets of lava dust and said 'Ah Japhy you taught me the final lesson of them all, you can't fall off a mountain.'" Kerouac's own distinctive style survives this transforming awareness in the typical exuberance of "buckets of lava dust." But the thematic point also claims our attention: the commonplace truth can have an uncommon force when we discover it ourselves, in our own acts. Another way to read this "final lesson" is to see it as an incidence of domesticating the sublime, turning the sacred space of the mountain into truth about one's own bodily existence. Such a mediation, between the domestic and the sublime, underpins much of the concern that animates *Turtle Island*.

Counterposed with Kerouac's lesson is an awareness that such a blissful trust in the local effects of gravity and the average slope of mountainsides can be misplaced. The larger dimensions of our awareness and our experience can sometimes distort and undermine our local efforts. Here is Michel Foucault, in a bleaker vein:

> I believe . . . that this particular idea of the "whole of society" derives from a utopian context. This idea arose in the Western world, within this highly individualized historical development that culminates in capitalism. To speak of the "whole of society" apart from the only form it has ever taken is to transform our past into a dream . . . But I believe that this . . . means imposing impossible conditions on our actions because this notion functions in a manner that prohibits the actualization, success, and perpetuation of these projects. "The whole of society" is precisely that which should not be considered except as something to be destroyed. And then, we can only hope that it will never exist again.[1]

Here a French intellectual speaks in part out of his profound dislike of the central power of the state and his hatred of totalitarianism, which he sees as a diseased utopian dream. But even allowing for the bias of his negative feelings, there is a truth here that presses on everyone who tries to imagine all of humankind in a single political or social scheme. I would suggest as an important qualification, however, that such universalist schemes are not exclusively the product of the capitalist epoch. All imaginative religious and political renderings of the cosmos, from the most "primitive" to the most historically devel-

1. From *Language, Counter-Memory, Practice: Selected Essays and Interviews*, trans. Donald Bouchard and Sherry Simon (Ithaca: Cornell University press, 1977), pp. 232–33.

oped, have drawn their boundaries so as to include "all," or at least all they thought to be valuable. As we will see, Snyder himself must mediate between the body-centered consciousness of Ray Smith and the past transformed into an all-encompassing, utopian dream that haunts Foucault.

Turtle Island

We can take Snyder's *Turtle Island* as the most complete expression of his political and poetic vision, not only because it is his most recent finished volume, but also because it contains the fullest mediations of the themes and concerns of all his work. I propose to look at the book as incorporating three mediations. First, *Turtle Island* serves Snyder with a chief metaphor for a physical environment and a utopian vision. As he puts it in the "Introductory Note," Turtle Island is the "old/new name for the continent, based on many creation myths of the people who have been living here for millenia." The metaphor of the continent floating on the back of a giant turtle serves as a cosmogonic emblem of archaic knowledge and future hopes: "Hark again to those roots, to see our ancient solidarity, and then to the work of being together on Turtle Island." This work, another version of the real work, extends beyond North America to "the earth, or cosmos even," because Turtle Island is another version of the "idea found world-wide" of a "serpent-of-eternity," the *uroboros* familiar to all students of world mythology. Turtle Island thus combines the immanent awareness of a space occupied for thousands of years with the historically transcendent space of the planet reimagined as the seat of the species.

Secondly, Snyder uses Turtle Island as a way of mediating between an ethics of responsibility and an ethics of ultimate ends. I take these terms from Max Weber's well-known essay "Politics as a Vocation" (1918).[2] Weber distinguishes between these two "fundamentally differing and irreconcilably opposed" senses of value, since those

2. In *From Max Weber: Essays in Sociology,* trans. and ed. H.H. Gerth and C. Wright Mills (New York: Oxford University Press, 1946), pp. 77–128.

who formulate or pursue ultimate ends are unlikely to take pragmatic consequences into consideration. But Weber is quick to add that the ethics of ultimate ends need not produce actions that deny or evade all consequences, and likewise the ethics of responsibility should not be equated with "unprincipled opportunism." Snyder includes in *Turtle Island* a section, called "Plain Talk," of prose essays, the most extended of which is "Four Changes." This essay contains "practical and visionary suggestions" and is the fullest statement in expository prose of Snyder's aims and beliefs. Here he advances several radical ideas: the world's population should be cut in half, alternative family structures should be explored, the world should be divided into "natural and cultural boundaries rather than arbitrary boundaries" (thereby eliminating nation-states and most existing political structures), we should seek a reliance on unobtrusive technologies and energy sources, and so forth. The arguments for each proposal mix appeals to scientific and technological fact and research with attacks on the ideology of consumption and private property. All of the proposals, however, are for a new ethics, and this new ethics stands in relation to our current ethical standards and behavior in a way that is based on both immediate responsibilities and ultimate ends.

The third major mediation in *Turtle Island* presents a sense of the lyric poem that has dominated literature for the last century and a half, together with a future model of the lyric poem as more committed to enhancing an awareness of cosmic scale and cosmic forces and the need of the community to heighten and preserve such awareness: "The common work of the tribe." The dominant current model of the lyric poem originated with the postromantic sense of the isolated artist and the autotelic theories of aesthetic experience. This model was made more or less canonic by such anthologies as F.T. Palgrave's *Golden Treasury* (1861) and by such critical studies, some generations later, as I.A. Richards's *Principles of Literary Criticism* (1925).[3] Snyder is indebted to this model, as is virtually every

3. See Christopher Clausen's essay on Palgrave in *Georgia Review* 34, 2 (Summer 1980): 273–89. Viewed from a radical perspective, this essay supports the view of Oakeshott mentioned above in Chapter 1.

postromantic poet, and his riprap poetics can be seen in part as an extreme development of one aspect of the art-lyric, the dictum against ornate or merely decorative imagery. But Snyder's more recent work is set against several other dicta of the art-lyric, chiefly the strict avoidance of intellectual content and didactic intentions. Snyder attempts to celebrate the common work of the tribe, and so his poetry has a didactic role, as well as a concern for group consciousness and social value (although more often of a desired rather than an actual sort) that mitigates against the art-lyric's concentration on the single, exacerbated sensibility. In a poem like "Anasazi," which opens *Turtle Island*, there is little or no trace of an observing subject or a lyrical ego; everything is subordinated to an almost phenomenological rendition of the Anasazi's tribal existence. More like an ethnographic field report than an art-lyric, this poem relies on an understood valuation that praises any social grouping that relates harmoniously to its physical environment. The ending of the poem blocks out in stark imagery the tribe's conditions of existence, and the ambiguity of reference equates the landscape with the tribe itself:

> trickling streams in hidden canyons
> under the cold rolling desert
>
> corn-basket   wide eyed
>   red baby
>   rock lip home,
>
> Anasazi

The "streams" can be the water that nourishes the Indians' crops or metaphorically the Indians themselves; the corn-basket can contain either the cereal that is the staple of their diet or their infants; their homes are made in and of the rock lip, the "clefts in the cliffs." The poem does not directly address any inner state or dramatize any emotional tension; it records and names rather than enacts or addresses its subject matter. It applies to us only insofar as we can see ourselves as products of, and preservers of, a physical environment.

94

Each of these three mediations helps to center Snyder's poetry and to support the other two; the mediation of poetic ends is, however, perhaps the most important. Snyder has talked about shamanistic songs and about the use of poetry and art that extends back to the Pleistocene era. Though the anthropological evidence is slim in these matters, there is a social use for poetry that extends beyond that of the art-lyric and the privatized reader. Some of this use function was once partly fulfilled by epic poetry, and today some have suggested it is fulfilled by advertising copywriters, who are the most successful, or at least widespread, mediators of our common dreams and our social reality. But Snyder returns to some of the functions of epic poetry while preempting the role of advertising. Here, from *The Old Ways*, is a description, written in 1975, of the new model of poetry Snyder envisions:

> We're just starting, in the last ten years here, to begin to make songs that will speak for plants, mountains, animals and children. When you see your first deer of the day you sing your salute to the deer, or your first red-wing blackbird—I saw one this morning! Such poetries will be created by us as we reinhabit this land with people who know they belong to it; for whom "primitive" is not a word that means past, but *primary*, and *future*. They will be created as we learn to see, region by region, how we live specifically (plant life!) in each place. The poems will leap out past the automobiles and TV sets of today into the vastness of the Milky Way (visible only when the electricity is turned down), to richen and humanize the scientific cosmologies. These poesies to come will help us learn to be people of knowledge in this universe in community with the other people—nonhuman included—brothers and sisters.

For me the key term here is "salute," for that is the mode of address in the Anasazi poem quoted above. Salutation involves recognition but also a well-wishing, a call to and for the forces of health and safety. Salutation, of course, also has a social dimension, and it communizes both its speaker and the person addressed. By this complex act of naming, well-wishing, and social placement, Snyder is less concerned with interior states than with environmental harmony. Learning to live "specifically . . . in each place" means knowing the plant life, knowing how the immediate physical environment makes available and uses its weather, soil, and other conditions to produce food, and this knowledge is necessary for the community to sustain its biological life as well as its cultural identity. Such localism and regionalism are not grounded in xenophobia or philistinism; rather they draw on and lead to a scientific understanding of the importance of place. Thus, Snyder's new poetry is as likely to include facts as it is to draw on so-called primitive or archaic knowledge and culture.

The second section of *Turtle Island* begins with a poem called "Facts," and in its ten numbered prose sentences it moves as far from the model of the art-lyric as would seem possible. Here are some samples:

1. 92% of Japan's three million ton import of soybeans comes from the U.S.
2. The U.S. has 6% of the world's population; consumes ⅓ the energy annually consumed in the world.
. . . .
6. General Motors is bigger than Holland.
7. Nuclear energy is mainly subsidized with fossil fuels and barely yields net energy.

These formulations can be further understood, beyond their self-explanatory factuality, in the larger contexts of Snyder's recurrent concerns. But such an integration into a larger vision does not make "Facts" a good poem. Certainly no argument will convince a reader who expects or desires an art-lyric to like "Facts." Thomas Parkinson has identified two modes in Snyder, one that is "measured, dramatic, definite . . . in design, formal, and contemplative," and another that is "fluent, wise, witty, meditative and hortatory." For Parkinson the first mode is clearly the best, while the second produces work that is "prepoetic."[4]

4. "The Theory and Practice of Gary Snyder," *Journal of Modern Literature* 2,3 (Winter 1971): 451. Parkinson's earlier essay, "The Poetry of Gary Snyder," *Southern Review* 4 (1968): 616–32, was largely positive and did much to win critical respect for Snyder, though now the piece seems rather thin. The later essay tries to deal with arguments against Snyder and shows a greater sense of the struggles involved in refining the vision.

Prepoetic, of course, would also describe most oral poetry, primitive chants, mantras, and other forms that, from the perspective of the art-lyric, lack the dramatic and contemplative features we associate with postromantic poetry. "Facts" can be seen as prepoetic not only because it lacks a dramatic or formal structure but because it clearly reads as prose and uses the language of mundane reality in nonstylized ways. But Snyder bids us to recall all the specificity of our world of prose; not every song can be a salutation, yet each poem can address a fact that informs the community about an essential aspect of its identity. By including the prepoetic (or the unpoetic, though this word has been largely outlawed since W.C. Williams objected to Wallace Stevens's use of it in describing Williams's poetry), Snyder at the very least implicitly acknowledges that a chant or song will not of itself alter social reality.

Another way to see "Facts" is to recognize that Snyder's ethics of responsibility does not get obscured by an ethics of ultimate ends, that the pressures and constraints of a very real social structure create an inescapable obligation to keep a vision alive with actual consequences.[5] Another poem, from the first section of *Turtle Island,* is closer to the art-lyric tradition, and its dramatic, anecdotal structure might be seen by a programmatic avant-gardist as old-fashioned. This is "I Went into the Maverick Bar," which vividly captures the despairing lack of social possibility that is a minor but important theme counterpointing Snyder's utopian vision.

> I went into the Maverick Bar
> In Farmington, New Mexico.
> And drank double shots of bourbon
> > backed with beer.
> My long hair was tucked up under a cap

5. See the essay by Altieri cited in Chapter II, footnote 2, above. Altieri's sense of reconciling prophet and seer overlaps with my sense of mediation in Snyder. For Altieri, the prophet's vision is communally directed while that of the seer is intensely private; for him Snyder's *Turtle Island* veers close to stereotype in some poems and is insufficiently charged with personal drama. In a sense, my argument about the new modes of poetry in Snyder is an attempt to address Altieri's telling criticism.

I'd left the earring in the car.
Two cowboys did horseplay
      by the pool tables,
A waitress asked us
      where are you from?
a country-and-western band began to play
"We don't smoke Marijuana in Muskokie"
And with the next song,
      a couple began to dance.

They held each other like in High School dances
      in the fifties;
I recalled when I worked in the woods
      and the bars of Madras, Oregon.
That short-haired joy and roughness—
      America—your stupidity.
I could almost love you again.

We left—onto the freeway shoulders—
      under the tough old stars—
In the shadow of bluffs
      I came back to myself,
To the real work, to
      "What is to be done."

The allusion to Lenin's revolutionary tract in the last line of the poem, along with the use of what is one of Snyder's key phrases, "the real work," poses this anecdote on an edge of ambiguity that in many ways resembles that prized in the art-lyric. Yet the ambiguity here—the unspecified commitment, the feelings of rejection and fear mingled with nostalgia and fondness—actually dissolves with the phrase "I came back to myself." Here Snyder realizes how far his values are from those of many of his ordinary fellow citizens, but he also realizes he must and will maintain those values. Unlike the art-lyric, which traditionally strives for an image of closure that focuses and yet heightens ambiguity, this poem closes with an opening vista of resolution to pursue an ethically formed, intellectually shaped goal.

The most important supposition of the art-lyric, namely that momentary emotion, heedless of larger consequences, has a self-justifying truth grounded in its very intensity, is here embodied in the flow of the verse. The dancing couple breaks in on the song celebrating repression, and this triggers the memories of work and class-affiliation, which are then shattered by an image impacted with contradictory emotional values ("short-haired joy and roughness"); this causes the speaker's consciousness to crest with a large abstract image, followed by the unconcealment of his emotional conflict. As a phrase, "I could almost love you again" refuses to indulge its lyric impulses, and instead the poem turns away from the immediately present community to a larger, less present, but more "real" commitment. So the verse, with its dashes and line breaks, not only enacts the process of discovery but also registers the speaker's self-denial and self-correction. The poem is about promise-within-failure, and it must take its recognition of the "common work of the tribe" away from the immediate source of its song.

Much of the tension present in "I Went into the Maverick Bar" pervades the whole of *Turtle Island.* The book is divided into four sections, three of poetry and one of prose. The sections of poetry—"Manzanita," "Magpie's Song," and "For the Children"—could respectively be considered a poetry of prayer and ritual, a poetry of instruction, and a poetry of hope. But this sort of classification will not hold firmly, and it is better to see each section as containing some poems from each of the three modes, though dominated by a specific set of concerns. Perhaps we can best see this organization, loose as it is, by looking closely at the shape and subjects of one section, noting some exceptions, and then glancing at the other two sections. In the section called "Manzanita," for example, the first two poems, "Anasazi" and "The Way West, Underground," are clearly salutations, the second being a poem about bears that recalls the Coyote poem that opened *The Back Country.* Then there is a poem that reads very like a doxology from a religious ritual: "Without," which argues that singing is "the proof of the power within." This poem announces one of the volume's chief themes, that all energy must be internally graceful in order to be truly powerful. Harmony relies on the path having "no / end in itself" but rather recircling in both inner and outer realms. The poem is written in simple language, virtually without imagery, and draws on the philosophical bent we saw in *Regarding Wave* (for which it could serve as a fitting epigraph). Other poems in this section, namely "The Great Mother," "No Matter, Never Mind," and "Prayer for the Great Family," resemble "Without," and together they can be read as Snyder's creation hymn and doxology. As a group they strongly influence the feeling of this section as one preoccupied with prayer and ritual. There is even an exorcism poem, "Spel Against Demons," which contributes to this feeling. In turn this feeling pervades a poem like "The Bath," with its refrain of *"This is our body"* and its description of an ideal erotic and familial union among Snyder, his wife, and his sons, Kai and Gen. The exceptions to this dominant mood are poems such as "I Went into the Maverick Bar," "Front Lines," and "The Call of the Wild." With a little ingenuity we could see these three poems as broken rituals, places where the "common work of the tribe" breaks down into alienation and mistrust. "Front Lines" recalls the poems in the "Logging" section of *Myths & Texts*, and here we see a

> bulldozer grinding and slobbering
> Sideslipping and belching on top of
> The skinned-up bodies of still-live bushes
> In the pay of a man
> From town.

Since Snyder has written this poem before, and generally better, the best reading of its inclusion here would argue that the problem of alienated labor has not gone away, and recognition of the problem is demanded even in a group of primarily celebratory poems.

The last two poems in the section contribute to the salutational atmosphere. The poem that lends the section its title, "Manzanita," is clearly a song of plant life that mediates between Coyote as a mythical figure and the plant itself, with its transformative power and its connections to the net of what Snyder calls "ethnobotany," the use of vegetative life in human culture. "The longer you look /

The bigger they seem," says the last stanza of the poem, describing the manzanita bushes. This poem then concludes by citing the etymology of the plant's name, "little apples." The final poem, "Charms," looks back to the mode of "The Song of the Taste" in *Regarding Wave,* but its subject is the "dreamlike perfection / of name-and-form" incorporated in female beauty. Snyder says that such beauty evokes "the Delight / at the heart of creation" and even avers that he could be "devastated and athirst with longing / for a lovely mare or lioness, or lady mouse." To the vegetable kingdom of "Manzanita" this poem exuberantly adds the animal kingdom, and where "Manzanita" is local and specific, "Charms" is universal; where the one celebrates the immediate physical environment, the other makes a hymn to a utopian sense of "another world," the Deva Realm as Snyder calls it. Read together the two lyrics not only help to complete our sense of Snyder's new poetry but they also show how the reinhabitation of the land will be aided by songs of knowledge and community. In a sense both of these poems are postpolitical, since they speak to a consciousness built of a total harmonization of man with nature and man with man.

As a section, then, "Manzanita" is heavily weighted with poems that salute principles of harmony and growth, though there are also poems, such as "Front Lines," that try to face up to the "Rot at the heart / In the sick fat veins of Amerika." The book's next section, "Magpie's Song," has several longer poems that seem concerned with conveying information, somewhat in the manner of Thoreau's natural historian who is content to let a fact flower into a truth. "Mother Earth: Her Whales," "Straight-Creek— Great Burn," and "The Hudsonian Curlew" take delight in descriptions of natural processes and rhythms and seek little metaphoric resonance beyond the awareness of immanent order and shapeliness. Again, this feeling is determined in part by the section's opening poem, "Facts," but it is also counterpointed by an ethical longing or predilection that arises in some of the shorter poems. I am thinking here of the conclusions to poems like "Ethnobotany" ("Taste all, and hand the knowledge down") and "Up

Branches of Duck River" ("hold it close / give it all away").
These ethical principles are, as I have suggested, sometimes versions of a Buddhist-like wisdom and sometimes a
practical field-knowledge. This particular mediation, between ultimate ends and local responses, has been a goal
of Snyder's poetry all along, of course, though it seems to
be more self-conscious and more aesthetically successful
in *Turtle Island* than in, say, *Riprap*. In this section's closing
poem, "Magpie's Song," Snyder begins with a specific
place and time and then alludes glancingly to the tutelary
or totemic figure of Coyote, but here the creature is seen
naturalistically. One might expect the following figure of
the magpie to also operate in a naturalistic manner, but
instead the poem ends with a message of hope and the
poet's integration of and with natural forces and his own
disciplined mind.

Six A.M.
Sat down on excavation gravel
by juniper and desert S.P. tracks
interstate 80 not far off
    between trucks
Coyotes—maybe three
        howling and yapping from a rise.

Magpie on a bough
Tipped his head and said,

> *"Here in the mind, brother*
> *Turquoise blue.*
> *I wouldn't fool you.*
> *Smell the breeze*
> *It came through all the trees*
> *No need to fear*
> *What's ahead*
> *Snow up on the hills west*
> *Will be there every year*
> *be at rest.*
> *A feather on the ground—*
> *The wind sound—*
>
> *Here in the Mind, Brother,*
> *Turquoise Blue"*

102

The magpie's instruction recalls the Rinzai sense of the mantras that are to be found in the patterns that result from natural forces: the blowing snow, the sounding wind. The poet has been fraternalized by this initiation or instruction scene, and the jeweled mind corresponds once more with the jeweled net of interconnected systems. The Amerindian West and the Buddhist East are brought together as the local and the cosmic open to one another.

The third and final section of poetry in *Turtle Island* is called "For the Children" and obviously deals with that new sense of the primitive that Snyder strives to establish, the primitive as both "primary" and "future." But the section also contains one of Snyder's boldest historical poems, "What Happened Here Before," which moves, in a little over three pages, from 300 million years ago to the present. The *here* refers to the area around Snyder's homestead in the Sierra Nevadas, and the poem ends with the challenge: "WE SHALL SEE / WHO KNOWS / HOW TO BE ." This challenge refers to the ethos of Snyder and the reinhabitants of Turtle Island, with their specific knowledge of county tax rates and local history as well as of their cosmic and prehistoric vistas, as opposed to the people who pilot the "military jets [that] head northwest, roaring, every dawn." Preceding this poem in the section is "Tomorrow's Song," which begins with the radical notion that because America "never gave the mountains and rivers, / trees and animals, / a vote," it has "slowly lost its mandate." This is Snyder's most challenging, most "untraditional" notion, that animals and trees should be represented by government and accorded rights. Part of his hope for the preservation of the wilderness and natural resources, this notion may also be seen as Snyder's final mediation between his reverence for nature and his socialist-humanist political vision. Snyder says that "We look to the future with pleasure" since we can "get power within / grow strong on less," and in this new political-natural order he imagines a people living on Turtle Island who will be "gentle and innocent as wolves / as tricky as a prince." By inverting the Hobbesian sense of man as predatory and by playfully invoking Machiavelli's *The Prince*,

Snyder redraws two of the Western political tradition's main metaphors and uses them to redefine what he means by being "At work and in our place." The real work is knowing what is to be done, but knowing also the ground—in all the senses of the word—on which it can be done. "Tomorrow's Song" is Snyder's salute to the future and contains one of his fullest descriptions of the ethos of Turtle Island.

The poem that lends its title to this last section of poetry, "For the Children," concludes with a simple testament of faith, a gesture that catches up elements of salutation and instruction to form a final set of ethical principles.

> In the next century
> or the one beyond that
> they say,
> are valleys, pastures,
> We can meet there in peace
> if we make it.
>
> To climb these coming crests
> one word to you, to
> you and your children:
> *Stay together*
> *learn the flowers*
> *go light*

Political community, reverence for nature, and an ascetic gracefulness—all of Snyder's values are reflected in these three injunctions. The simplicity of the diction and the images recalls Blake, and the whole tradition of the literary ballad, in which a sophisticated poet adopts a simple framework to say something that is at once primitive and essential. Snyder's "one word" is the equivalent of what Kerouac called the "final lesson," and in each case the sublime is domesticated, brought home by bodily knowledge and mental harmony.

Taken together, and with the remarkable prose essays as well, the three sections of poetry in *Turtle Island* form a whole that advances Snyder's work well beyond the objectivist poetics of the early books and the political suppositions of *Earth House Hold*. Supplemented with the essays of *The Old Ways*, some of which are contemporary with *Turtle Island*, Snyder's vision is as full and distinctive as that of any of his contemporaries, including the slightly earlier generation of Lowell, Berryman, and Jarrell. Only Olson, I believe, compares with him in terms of a mythic imagination, and only Levertov has as broad and deep a political consciousness. But can Snyder claim for his art (or can his readers claim on his behalf) any authority other than that of the aesthetic realm? Take his notion that trees and animals should be represented in Congress. While this neatly ties together his ecological awareness and his political concerns, can the average reader see it as anything but an amusing conceit? Perhaps we can glimpse through this "literary" notion, this play with metaphors and contexts, a twitting of the serious tradition of representative democracy. Or can we better see it as a serious critique of representational government if we realize that banks and corporations command a share of representative power in our legislatures, and they are no more capable of speaking for themselves, without human mediation, than are trees and animals? If humans can find a way to define the rights of a corporation, why can they not do the same for the forest?

As for *Turtle Island* as a literary work, its language goes against the grain of several canonic tenets of modernism, and it flies in the face of once fashionable styles such as confessionalism. Like much genuinely innovative work, Snyder's poetry resorts to some quite ancient strategies and rhetorical gestures. Without the resplendent imagery of neo-surrealism, or the tight dramatic irony of academic poetry, or the display of an exacerbated sensibility, Snyder has reduced and yet enlarged the range of the lyric poem. But only a reader with at least a political awareness, if not a like-minded political will, can extensively respond to that range. Snyder has not solved the problem (how could he?) that animated so much of the theory of the autotelic art-lyric in the first place, namely, should not the extra-literary considerations of political or ethical belief be separated from the judgment of a poem on purely literary grounds? Snyder's work implicitly rejects the autotelic, formalist solution which said that only strictly structural and technical criteria should determine the worth of a poem, "as poem." This rejection is etched in the apparent lack of formal expertise in much of his poetry (though in fact his prosody can be quite sophisticated if judged from a nontraditional vantage point). Whether his language use can bring about a broad revival of, or even limited respect for, such forms as a poetry of salutation or instruction is an intriguing possibility. As early as the 1952 "Lookout's Journal" in *Earth House Hold*, Snyder asked:

> —If one wished to write poetry of nature, where an audience?
> Must come from the very conflict of an attempt to articulate
> the vision   poetry and nature in our time.
> (reject the human; but the tension of
> human events, brutal and tragic, against
> a non-human background? like Jeffers?)

It is to the credit of *Turtle Island*, and the whole of Snyder's work, that he has not rejected the human, and indeed has avoided Jeffers's solution by refusing to subordinate the human to the nonhuman. On the other hand, what separates Snyder from many traditional poets is his refusal to appropriate the nonhuman (or natural) realm as no more than a dramatic or illustrative backdrop to the "tension of human events." This is what gives Snyder a legitimate claim to be operating as much outside or beyond the contexts of traditional literary values as any other contemporary poet. What *Turtle Island* finally mediates is the tension in mythical speculation that sees the world as supported and yet free-floating. Literature in such a mediation can try to be both self-grounded and ethically normative. But no modern poet would ever think such a dual burden could be easily lightened. Snyder says in the closing poem of *Turtle Island* that

> A Mind Poet
> Stays in the house.
> The house is empty
> And it has no walls.
> The poem
> Is seen from all sides,

Everywhere,
At once.

We have to realize the "house" is both the cosmos and the imagination, and that a poem whose perspective is pan-optic and omnipresent can be understood both as an art-lyric poised on the vanishing point of self-reflective irony and as a cosmic hymn of all-embracing belief. Here Snyder's vision, or at least his desire for a healing vision, is as full as possible.

*   *   *

As a mediating force, the master metaphor of Turtle Island is both cultic and universal. As a cultic symbol, Turtle Island belongs to a category of mythmaking that resembles what Robert Ellwood has defined as "excursus religion." Snyder does not propose himself as a leader of this new social group, nor does he discuss how its leadership would function or develop.[6] What we can see as positive in Turtle Island is thus likely to remain idealized and even mystical, for despite Snyder's emphasis on practical knowledge and deep-seated awareness of the environment, most readers will see the metaphor as essentially opposed to indus-trialized, urbanized society. And, as Ellwood argues, one of the chief features of excursus religion is its oppositional

6. One important question that remains undiscussed in Snyder criti-cism is why there is apparently little room in his work for any soteriologi-cal myth, not just as such a myth is based on a belief in Christ but as it is based on any idea of a "personal savior." Snyder seems little interested in heroes of any sort, except those who can be addressed generically, for example the American Indian. Throughout his work Snyder praises per-sonal effort and somatically centered values, but he almost never ideal-izes historical individuals or personal friends. Part of this is clearly due to his Buddhist background, both as cause and effect, since the Buddha is in one sense soteriological, but in other important senses there are many buddhas. This raises the question of antithetical criticism: it would be (theoretically) possible to write useful and important criticism about an artist by considering what his or her vision does *not* entail or even allow to be treated. I would suggest that in Snyder's case this absence derives from the truly communal quality of his vision, another way of saying he is more a mythic than a lyric poet, perhaps. (On this point, see *The Real Work*, p. 20.) Nowhere else is his sharp difference from confessional or neo-surrealist poetry more apparent than in this "missing" concern.

character.[7] As an excursus religion, Turtle Island shares with similar socioreligious movements not only the opposition to dominant social structures but other important features as well. Two such features, discussed by Ellwood in connection with the Shakers, are an emphasis on body-centered or "sensorimotor expression" and symbolic pluralism, an acceptance of many spiritual orders rather than one central deity. We have already seen how both of these concerns are crucial to Snyder's vision and need not linger on them here except to say that Snyder can be seen as part of a long tradition of American spirituality. It is even possible to view this spiritual tradition as determining Snyder's political vision, or at least being of equal importance, in our reading of his poetry, with more explicitly social issues.

Many of the examples of excursus religion that Ellwood discusses either began with or eventuated in opposition to the dominant social structures and values, and this opposition often took the form of a loosely communitarian or socialist alternative. Linked to this political desire was an embrace of some form of Neoplatonic belief in parallel spiritual and physical realms. What seems to link these two commitments is a sense that the organized socioreligious structure had, by its hierarchy, its static ritual, and its emphasis on order and seemliness, lost its ability to vivify its beliefs. The other, higher realm could not be reached. However, in nineteenth-century America, when such groups as the Transcendentalists, the Shakers, and the Spiritualists were most prominently active, excursus religion often became allied with Enlightenment or progressive ideas. This may seem contradictory to those with only a later and somewhat superficial view of the era's spiritual movements. And it is true that the unorthodox groups often employed unorthodox means, relying on seances, personal ecstasy, mesmeric practices, automatic writing, and other "unscientific" means to contact the spiritual

7. Robert S. Ellwood, Jr., *Alternative Altars: Unconventional and Eastern Spirituality in America* (Chicago: University of Chicago Press, 1979), p. 121. This study includes a discussion of Snyder, but the entire book is of great interest.

realm. (Of course what passed as scientific even one hundred and fifty years ago is quite different from what we would accept today.) Perhaps equally surprising is the affinity some unorthodox cults felt for the rituals and beliefs of the American Indian. This ability to combine ideas usually associated with the apparently opposing traditions of scientific, materialistic progress and atavistic, superstitious religion resulted in large measure from the oppositional origins of the sects and cults. In pitting themselves against the orthodoxy they perceived to be stultifying and unresponsive, excursus religions sought solace and clarification in any body of thought or ritual that challenged the commonplace and the entrenched.

Snyder's mediations share much with the spirit of this nineteenth-century tradition; perhaps most important of all is a belief that those who desire spiritual truth and political revival must look back to a broader and more humane sense of health and growth as well as forward to a more informed and balanced use of social capacities. The religion of Paleolithic shamanism and the utopianism of postindustrial science can, and in Snyder's view must, be brought together if the current impasse is not to result in irreversible ecological disaster. The revolutionary need to draw on a past, even one that existed prior to official versions, and the desire to map a future, in the face of overwhelming institutional resistance, must eventually be supported by some totalizing vision. Turtle Island is a base of support and is itself unsupported; as Snyder says at the end of "Four Changes," "Knowing that nothing need be done, is where we begin to move from." I think such a formulation rests on a belief in total freedom mixed equally with an almost fatalistic, Buddhist negation of will. What Snyder calls for is a redemption of the entire historical realm, a purchase on a purposive future, and what every revolutionary and spiritual prophet calls for, namely, a new sense of what it means to be human. To make such a call precedes any scheme for achieving such results. What is more, the very calls may sometimes make any results supererogatory. The call is everything for some visionaries, since what they might find in the area of practical results would always be disappointing.

I do not think Snyder is such a visionary, as the proposals in "Four Changes" make clear. But at the same time legislative representation for deers and Douglas firs is not an immediate prospect. Closer to more traditional aesthetic aims lies Snyder's new sense of the self. Many modernist writers, such as Rimbaud or Lawrence, have either called for a new structuring of the psyche or proceeded as if one were imminent. Snyder also has such a sense. Perhaps its essential feature, which is really an extension of several romantic ideas, is that the natural wilderness and the unconscious are analogous. As Snyder puts it in "The Wilderness," one of the prose essays in *Turtle Island:*

> There are many things in Western culture that are admirable. But a culture that alienates itself from the very ground of its own being—from the wilderness outside (that is to say, wild nature, the wild, self-contained, self-informing ecosystems) and from that other wilderness, the wilderness within—is doomed to a very destructive behavior, ultimately perhaps self-destructive behavior.

After this passage Snyder goes on to give examples of environmental destruction from both Eastern and Western cultures and implicitly makes the point that he is talking about something endemic to civilization, not just to European culture. But if such destructiveness is so widespread and apparently universal, many either will need to identify it or will despair of eliminating or correcting it. However, Snyder avoids any myth of original sin or fallenness, just as he avoids misanthropy or historical despair. This very avoidance is what many will see as the crucial limitation in Snyder's thought or in his mythical imagining. But at this crux about all we can say is that he louder sings for every tatter of his mortal dress. What Snyder proposes as his new version of the self is an analogue of the "self-informing ecosystem," so that the revolutionary psyche is viewed as a dynamic equilibrium of parts that are themselves parts of yet other systems, all working in harmonious interdependence. This passage is from "Reinhabitation," in the *The Old Ways:*

110

Is not the purpose of all this living and studying the achievement of self-knowledge, self-realization? How does knowledge of place help us know the Self? The answer, simply put, is that we are all composite beings, not only physically but intellectually, whose sole identifying individual feature is a particular form or structure changing constantly in time. There is no "self" to be found in that, and yet oddly enough, there is. Part of you is out there waiting to come into you, and another part of you is behind you, and the "just this" of the ever-present moment holds all the transitory selves in its mirror. The Avatamsaka ("Flower Wreath") jeweled-net-interpenetration — ecological — systems — emptiness — consciousness tells us, no self-realization without the Whole self, and the whole self is the whole thing.

Thus, knowing who and where are intimately linked. There are no limits to the possibilities of the study of *who* and *where*, if you want to go "beyond limits"—and so, even in a world of biological limits, there is plenty of open mind-space to go out into.

The replacement of the actual, physical frontier by "inner space" is a theme common to many writers and discussed by several critics.[8] What is more pertinent here is how Snyder has recontained the sense of the void that haunted him at the end of *Myths & Texts* and at the same time integrated his sense of the powers of the mind and the demands of place. By seeing the mind—actually the self, since what we have here is a very disciplined, structured, and culturally shaped sense of consciousness—as an emptiness that provides an opening into infinitude and escapes the closure of nature (even "wild nature") while it yet is shaped by nature, Snyder is led to a new sense of self. The flux of nature exists as a self-informing system; this is the basic claim of all ecology. Likewise with the self of the psyche, which is flux and form, past and whole, inner and outer, moment and mirror. The world and the earth of Heidegger resemble the who and the where of Snyder, and the space of the mind can be gone *out* into, so that mind is locatable not only in the interior life but in the

8. One example would be the essay "Cross the Border, Close the Gap," in Leslie Fiedler's *Collected Essays* (New York: Stein & Day, 1971).

understood environment as well. Turtle Island encompasses Snyder's other figures—the kiva, the jeweled net, the back country—not only because of its greater ecological finesse but also because of its more developed sense of the self.

Mountains and Rivers Without End

For twenty years or more, off and on, Snyder has been writing a long poem that in many ways embodies his sense of a new self. The work is called *Mountains and Rivers Without End,* and to date he has published seven sections of it in one volume, and five uncollected sections in various journals.[9] I would like to look at a few of the seven sections included in the 1977 volume, which give a fairly clear idea of the way the poem is built, though obviously a definitive study will have to wait until Snyder completes this ambitious work. The most obvious feature of the work so far is that it is clearly a poem of process. With its loose verse forms, shifting contexts, inclusion of apparently heterogeneous and sometimes recondite material, and a compendium of styles and levels of diction, *Mountains and Rivers* has clear precedents in Pound's *Cantos,* Williams's *Paterson,* and Olson's *Maximus.* Speaking impressionistically, however, I think it is closest to *Paterson,* for its structure has the feel of partially developed incidents (where Pound tends to be most allusive in his narrative), and it feels more indigenous and "folksy" (where Olson often deals with esoterica and an almost academic range of reference). The sense of process is situ-

9. The five sections appeared as "Three Worlds / Three Realms / Six Roads," in *Poetry* (December 1966); "The Hump-Backed Flute Player," *Coyote's Journal* 9; "Down," *Iowa Review* 1, 4 (1970); "The California Water Plan," *Clear Creek* 8 (November 1971); and "Ma," *Coyote's Journal* 10. Bob Steuding, in *Gary Snyder* (Boston: Twayne, 1976), quotes briefly from an unpublished section. He also quotes Snyder as having said that the whole work will close with a section organized around a remark of a mountain man to the effect that "Where there ain't no Indians that's where you find them thickest." Among other things, *Mountains* is clearly part of Snyder's epic of the great subculture, a celebration of all the otherwise voiceless hopes for plenitude.

ated within a form, though one that is based on a loose metaphoric association with the Chinese scroll paintings. Here is a description of the poem from Japhy Rider, Kerouac's fictional version of Snyder, which seems generally accurate, not only about the poem's title but about its structure as well.

> "Know what I'm gonna do? I'll do a new long poem called 'Rivers and Mountains without End' and just write it on and on on a scroll and unfold on and on with new surprises and always what went before forgotten, see, like a river, or like one of them real long Chinese silk paintings that show two little men hiking in an endless landscape of gnarled old trees and mountains so high they merge with the fog in the upper silk void. I'll spend three thousand years writing it, it'll be packed full of information on soil conservation, the Tennessee Valley Authority, astronomy, geology, Hsuan Tsung's travels, Chinese painting theory, reforestation, oceanic ecology and food chains."

The combination of flux and form here is analogous to the new sense of self outlined in "Re-inhabitation." But another pleasure in reading *Mountains* comes from its complex sense of space. Space in Chinese scroll paintings obviously differs from that of Western art, especially perspectival painting. In the scroll the space is relatively unbounded, because of the continuity of the scenes as the scroll is unrolled. There is also the sense of void or totally negative space, what Japhy calls the "upper silk void," that embodies the Buddhist sense of all reality being unsupported and hence understood only in the relationships between things, as opposed to the Western metaphysical notions of solidity and substance. This sense of space is achieved, in part, through the play between foreground and background, the use of human figures ("two little men") seen against large and almost overpowering natural forms ("an endless landscape of . . . mountains so high they merge with the fog"). This particular spatial sense is extremely apt for Snyder's speaker in poems like "Bubbs Creek Haircut," "The Elwha River," and "Night Highway Ninety-Nine." The political spirit in these poems is decidedly democratic, but there is also the spirit of the outrider, the lonely observer who drifts from place to place but with enough experience in various forms of manual labor that he can quickly empathize with the local people he meets. In brief, the poem's politics are like Whitman's, adhesive, fluid, fraternal.

As for the structure that keeps each section from being totally random, it often depends on an idea or image clustered around certain associations (some spatial, some temporal), so that a very tenuous central metaphor is searched out through a series of metonymic ties. Take "Bubbs Creek Haircut," for instance. It begins with Snyder getting a haircut in San Francisco prior to a hiking trip to Bubbs Creek. Next door to the barbershop is a Goodwill store where he will buy second-hand clothes and supplies for the trip. The poem links images triggered by the barber chair, the haircut, and the hiking trip to form a meditation on discarded things, natural forms, headpieces (the green hat Snyder wears allows a driver to recognize the poet from a hitchhiking experience two years previously), and the tenuousness of memory and existence. Here is a fairly typical passage, where the play of forms and connections mingles with the coarse humor of a logger (as later in the poem McCool gives Snyder a similar message for Moorehead):

> hiking up Bubbs Creek saw the trail crew tent
> in a scraggly grove of creekside lodgepole pine
>   talked to the guy, he says
> "If you see McCool on the other trailcrew over there
> tell him Moorehead says to go to hell."
> late snow that summer. Crossing the scarred bare
>   shed of Forester Pass
>   the winding rock-braced switchbacks
> dive in snowbanks, we climb on where
>   pack trains have to dig or wait.
> a half iced-over lake, twelve thousand feet
>   its sterile boulder bank
> but filled with leaping trout:
>   reflections wobble in the
> mingling circles always spreading out
>   the crazy web of wavelets makes sense
>   seen from high above.

                the realm of fallen rock.
        a deva world of sorts—it's high
                        it is a view that few men see, a point
                bare sunlight
                on the spaces
        empty sky
                        moulding to fit the shape of what ice left
        of fire-thrust, or of tilted, twisted, faulted
                                cast-out from this lava belly globe.

This poem was first published in 1961, and it obviously
anticipates the concerns of *Regarding Wave,* which appeared almost ten years later. Since Snyder composed
Mountains during the same span of time that saw the publication of his other five complete volumes of poetry, we
should not be surprised to find motifs and concerns, even
specific phrases, appearing in both places. But *Mountains*
seems to read in places like an anticipation of later work
and in other places like a reversion to earlier concerns and
styles. Here, the sentence that begins "Crossing the scar-
red bare / shed" ripples with assonance and even one ter-
minal rhyme, and it recalls the objectivist poetics of
Riprap, even down to the image of the trout, which echoes
a passage from "A Walk" in *The Back Country*. Thematically, the key passage is "the crazy web of wavelets
makes sense / seen from high above," since the whole
section is about abstraction, in the sense of experiential
moments connecting with one another to reveal a pattern
that is not immediately apparent. The haircut itself is an
anticipatory act, a making ready for a future plan, and it is
joined to the purchase of secondhand material from the
Goodwill store, a link with the past. Thus the spaces of the
poem—the atmosphere of the barbershop and the Goodwill, the landscape of Bubbs Creek, the hitchhiking there
and back—intersect and overlap without any real fixed
perspective, unless it be the haircut itself. The poem begins with the line, "High ceilingd and the double mirror,"
setting the scene in the barbershop, and it ends almost
four hundred lines later with

        out of the memory of smoking pine
    The lotion and the spittoon glitter rises

Chair turns and in the double mirror waver
The old man cranks me down and cracks a chuckle

"your Bubbs Creek haircut, boy."

The double mirrors here are like the self that both holds and spills images even as it connects them. Syntactically, the end of the haircut rises from the smoking pine odor of the trip that took place after the time in the barbershop. Of course, the opening haircut could be a flashback to a much earlier haircut prior to the hiking trip, but in any case the poem hangs suspended between the beginning of some haircut and the end of another, or the same one. The framing device, as in Chinese scroll paintings, is also a transitional device, indeed an "unframing" device since in the very form of being the container, the haircut serves to free or dissolve the "crazy web of wavelets" of memory and association.

Other sections from *Mountains* plainly utilize a shifting sense of time and place while still being formed by some organizing principle. "Night Highway Ninety-nine" begins with a song celebrating the open road, and it strings along a series of hitchhiking incidents, all of which occur on the road from Seattle to San Francisco. As with "Six Years" from *The Back Country*, where six years in Japan were condensed into a twelve-section poem built on the months of the calendar, "Night Highway" may condense several trips into one north-south journey. Thematically, this poem is about the grid of traveled space, with its seemingly endless vistas and its curious crossings; as one couplet puts it, "The road that's followed goes forever; / In half a minute crossed and left behind." As in "Bubbs Creek Haircut," framing devices spring up only to fade or shift, as drivers, vistas, destinations, cars, and bits of conversation connect and disconnect in a flux of imagery. In "The Market," Snyder presents a kaleidoscope of sights and sounds from the "heart of the city," the farmers' market of San Francisco. The second part of the poem is a reflection on economics and the mechanics of trade and exchange relations. By listing a few dozen items, each shown as equal to some other item (equal in price, or exchange, and so, as determined by the system, equal in value), Snyder wittily plays with the illogic of economic transactions, where "one hour explaining power steering / equals two big crayfish," and their essential role in human interaction and social structure. Labor in the market is both alienated and yet oddly rehumanized, for the market (unlike the market relations of a strictly cash economy or a trade in commodity options) has a flesh-and-blood dimension. It is the scene of desire ("if the belly be fed" says the key line) and carnival-like upheaval of social hierarchy. Unlike Galway Kinnell's "The Avenue Bearing the Initial of Christ," however, Snyder's welter of impressions has no transcendent plan, other than the recurrent and ever-present needs and products of the human community.

Perhaps the most ambitious, and the most challenging, section of *Mountains* is "The Blue Sky." Here the central image recalls the "Turquoise Blue" of the "Magpie's Song" in *Turtle Island.* At one level this image represents the Buddhist void, the metaphysical nonpresence that throws the mind back to the relationships between things, and back to its own emptiness, rather than letting it seek comfort in some real or ideal substratum in which and on which physical phenomena exist. At another level, the blue sky is the utopian future, a space of healing existence looked over by "Old Man Medicine Buddha."

> Thinking on Amitabha in the setting sun,
>   his western paradise
>   impurities flow out away, to west,
>   behind us, rolling.
> planet ball forward turns into the "east"
> is rising,
> azure,
> two thousand light years ahead
>
> Great Medicine Master;
> land of blue.

This future state is given an ecological definition in another poem from *Turtle Island,* where the condition of maximum biological diversity produces stability, and this is called "climax." By being able to "draw on the mind's /

stored richness," the evolutionary process can be brought to yet higher stages. But evolution is always pointed toward climax; climax is a culmination that can easily become the setting for a new burst of forms or new diversity in the "biomass." In this sense, the natural world, the mind, and aesthetic experience (in the metaphor of a scroll painting with its form-in-flux) all become analogous. Here is how Snyder describes the process in "Poetry Community & Climax" (1978), one of his most recent essays from *The Real Work* and the most developed integration of his thought:

> Turning away from grazing on the "immediate biomass" of perception, sensation, and thrill; and re-viewing memory, internalized perception, blocks of inner energies, dreams, the leaf-fall of day to day consciousness, liberates the energy of our own sense-detritus. Art is an assimilator of unfelt experience, perception, sensation, and memory for the whole society. When all that comfort of feeling and thinking comes back to us then, it comes not as a flower, but—to complete the metaphor—as a mushroom: the fruiting body of the buried threads of mycelia that run widely through the soil, and are intricately married to the root hairs of all the trees. "Fruiting"—at that point—is the completion of the work of the poet, and the point where the artist or mystic re-enters the cycle: gives what she or he has done as nourishment, and as spore or seed spreads the "thought of enlightenment", reaching into personal depths for nutrients hidden there, back to the community. The community and its poetry are not two.

This elaborate metaphor for cultural activity nicely delineates the structure of *Mountains* as well as brings together the spirit of attentiveness and slow purpose that animates Snyder's thought in the realms of nature and community life. The final product, the mushroom or poem, might not be spectacular or dramatically charged, yet it becomes the culmination of several interlocking processes and thus serves as a sign of health in that the process of *its* growth depends on and demonstrates all those others that support it.

The role of the self in this passage is intriguing, for again we see that the self is both process and product ("compost of feeling and thinking"), reminiscent of the familiar stable ego of nineteenth-century realism, but also drawing on a sense of psychic dynamism developed during the modernist era. *Mountains* is Snyder's most personal poetry, even more so than the autobiographical poems in *The Back Country,* but it has much of the communal scale that we saw him striving for in *Turtle Island*. Again, the work does not fit neatly into any format of stylistic growth, given the temporal scheme of its composition, but it does register a very subtle sense of thought and self and song. Too far from completion to be called Snyder's masterpiece, *Mountains* remains full of promise and bids fair to join other similar modernist epics in being very much part of the tale of the tribe.

IV. Some Closing Thoughts

> We can say that no connection exists between our liberal
> educated class and the best of the literary mind of our time.
> And this is to say that there is no connection between the
> political ideas of our educated class and the deep places of
> the imagination.
>
> —Lionel Trilling, *The Liberal Imagination* (1950)

During the second week of February 1983, what the
New York Times described as a "dazzling array of novelists,
movie stars, directors, and intellectuals" was hosted by
the Socialist government of François Mitterand in an attempt to discover how cultural issues and values could
address the world economic crisis. One might easily wonder if such participants as William Styron, Mary McCar-
thy, Graham Greene, and Susan Sontag have thought
more about the radical reimagining of European political
visions than has Gary Snyder. At the same time another
conference, of a decidedly different political persuasion,
was held in New York City, hosted by the Committee for
the Free World and including speakers such as Irving
Kristol, Norman Podhoretz, and Joseph Epstein. The latter asked the audience a pointed question: "Suddenly
American literature, contemporary American literature,
seems rather lackluster, a bit beside the point, less than
first rate, even though American political power is still
great. Why?"[1] Undaunted by his own lack of chronological
precision (was "suddenly" a matter of weeks or days?),
Epstein goes on to opine that the contemporary writing
scene is "rife with writers whose chief stock in the trade of

1. *New York Times,* 14 February 1983. The crucial word, of course, is
great. Some would understand this to mean extensive and physically
powerful, while others would see it in a moral or even spiritual dimension. I would argue that such power is great in the first sense but increasingly less so in the second. This paradox is what is often behind the
literature that Epstein may have in mind. Poets as otherwise different as
Snyder and Robert Lowell reflect this paradox in their work, a paradox I
would characterize as centered on the theme of blocked power.

ideas is a fairly crude sort of anti-Americanism." It is safe to assume Epstein would find Snyder's work "lack-luster," or worse, and see anti-Americanism as the cause of its being "less than first rate." I would argue that Snyder, though not invited to the French conference, could better address its theme than a large majority of those who attended and that his poetry and prose are indeed "a bit beside the point," if the point is defined as how the writer's excellence stems from his being pro-American.

The rejection of Snyder by the more visibly organized institutions of cultural and political policymaking is hardly surprising. Indeed, the French government and the Committee for the Free World can almost be excused for not thinking to invite any contemporary American poets, since many of them are both nonpolitical and antisocial, if only in a rather codified way. Snyder's attempt to radically question and reformulate the main metaphors of political thought, lyric form, and individual self-definition sets him apart from most of his peers, but such distinctiveness is difficult to appreciate. To revert to the question that opened this book, I would say that Snyder does attempt to step outside the main traditions of Western European po-litical philosophy, but he does so in ways that have impor-tant traditional supports and precedents. A deconstruc-tionist reading of Snyder might show that his is the role of an outrider, a scapegoat, and yet a medicine man, a chan-ter of cures. Furthermore, in his work "nature" and "the common work of the tribe" could be construed to outline both the insight and the blindness central to his vision. The tribe is the natural saving remnant of the species, yet it has its political and ethical value conferred on it by its very rejection of the dominant tradition, its "unnatural" status viewed from the standpoint of common sense or cultural committees. What is common or natural is never a given, nor is it ever defined without some political power and repressive exclusion being exercised.

Nevertheless, there is a limit to the extent to which even deconstruction can treat political structures as no more than rhetorical systems. Part of Snyder's value as a political visionary rests, I would argue, on his recalling of inescapable realities, such as the absolute limit to the supply of fossil fuels. As the poem "Facts" implicitly argues, all our work, all our commonality must take place within certain undeniable bounds. True, within such bounds rhetoric has an important, even crucial task. Even the decision about which facts are most urgently in need of recall arguably counts as a rhetorical decision. But Snyder himself does not share the literary intellectual's penchant for seeing all questions as questions of language. At the same time, Snyder offers a political program, most explicitly in the "Four Changes" section of *Turtle Island,* that is unlikely to find immediate or widespread backing. The sad truth is that since the late 1960s and early 1970s, with the subsidence of political activism associated with the antiwar and pro-ecology movements, Snyder's work has seemed less and less "relevant" (always a two-edged word) to many readers. The yet sadder truth is that none of the local facts or the larger issues of his work is any the less valid. Even poetry must suffer the vicissitudes of a consumption-oriented society. The searching reader may ask whether Snyder's eclipse, relative to the widespread readership he enjoyed ten years ago, is the result of the failure of his rhetoric or the realities of his audience.

This is a difficult question, obviously, and I have no ready answer for it. If, for example, Snyder's *Mountains and Rivers* and *Earth House Hold* are indeed attempts to tell the tale of the tribe, and such a tale is doomed by the nature of our political and social realities to be partial and inchoate, then Snyder's attempt can be regarded as foolhardy or noble. In purely aesthetic terms, terms that I have myself suggested are not completely sufficient in judging Snyder, these books are rich, varied, demanding, and consistent. In aesthetic terms, we should not ask for much more. Beyond the aesthetic dimensions, however, Snyder's poetry must be submitted to whatever standards one can tolerably apply to it. Here I would argue that the poetry and essays are drawn from a deep political imagination, of a sort that has been generally absent from our culture, as well as our literature, for some time. To ask that

122

such a political imagination again be given serious hearing, both within and apart from literary art, is to ask for both the improbable and necessary redefinition of our political discourse.

One way to measure the depth of Snyder's political vision is to compare it with other critical reassessments of the main traditions of European political philosophy. One such reassessment is Hannah Arendt's *The Human Condition* (1958). Though Snyder's work does not stand comparison in terms of detailed argument or consistency of development with the whole of Arendt's writing about politics, his poetry does offer interesting comparisons with this one book. Arendt's three main terms—labor, work, and action—correspond respectively to the biological metabolism, the artificial world of manufactured objects, and the nonmaterial activity between people, all of which go to make up the condition of any political life. In Snyder's vision the emphasis is very heavily weighted on the first and third of these realms of action. In part this is due to Snyder's primitivism, his refusal or reluctance to value the world of mechanical industry that today dominates the realm of human work. One of Snyder's key metaphors, interbirth, obviously stresses the metabolic interdependence of the human and natural orders and indicates the poet's willingness to go outside more traditional vocabularies in order to make his claims. Recall, however, in *The Back Country,* that a poem like "The Firing," with its sacralized sense of the art of the potter, shows Snyder's respect for "work," at least on the level of handcrafts. Clearly it is the modern sense of industrial mass production that Snyder rejects. Arendt herself is far from being laudatory about the world of production lines and automated manufacture, but her way of assessing it, in terms of its development and human significance, shows clearly how she is much more a political analyst than Snyder. By concentrating on very real issues, such as the liquid breeder reactor, Snyder shows he is conversant with the problems of industrial development, but he is less able to create a step-by-step program to answer the seemingly inevitable onward rush of such potentially disastrous developments. Moreover, the impression remains, not altogether unfounded, that he would like to do away with the realm of work and have people exist in simple communes devoted to small-scale agriculture. (A balancing note, however, is in *The Old Ways* where Snyder has a delightful essay on San Francisco, mixing topograpnical description and personal reminiscence. The essay shows how valuable and stimulating urban life can be for people.)

Another point of contrast between Snyder and Arendt is their use of privileged terms, and more specifically the sort of axiological etymology both engage in. In Arendt's book the derivation and clarification of classical terms such as *polis, urbs,* and *homo faber* serve a normative function for her discourse. Snyder's use of *kiva, tribe,* and *Turtle Island* has an analogous function, but we can also see that the difference in vocabularies is more than superficial or tactical. Such differences lie at the heart of what separates the two writers, and only by abstracting from their arguments can the reader see them as engaged in similar efforts. But such abstraction betrays the force of both arguments, since Snyder and Arendt intend their wordplay in the most serious possible way. As was argued above, Snyder's development of interest in the abstract patterning of paratactic metaphor in *Regarding Wave* signaled an important new stage in his poetic. But this abstraction was in no wise intended to deny the importance of the local and rooted senses of political value, as *Turtle Island* makes clear in many instances.

However, despite the differences between words like *polis* and *kiva,* Arendt's thought overlaps Snyder's in at least one important instance: her distinction between earth and world. I would argue she borrows these terms from Heidegger (unaccountably, however, her book never mentions his work, even though she had earlier been a close student of his) and uses them in the sense I tried to apply to *Myths & Texts.* Snyder does not employ these terms as such, but I think much of his political vision rests on a sense of "earth" as subtending "world," earth being a realm of prior value (pace the deconstructionists) that supports the more immediate social realm of human collectivity. The kiva, for example, is Snyder's way of mediating, or rather dramatizing the inescapable mediation, between earth and world. For Arendt, "though we live now, and probably always will, under the earth's conditions, we are not mere earth-bound creatures." Snyder's agreement with this formulation would, I suspect, be qualified. For him it is "mind" that enables us to escape from *mere* earth-boundedness, rather than any specific material development such as space technology or a soil-free agriculture made possible by advanced scientific means. The use of *probably* in Arendt's formulation suggests that a small detail may cover a potentially large distinction in temperaments and beliefs.

Arendt uses the metaphor of an "Archimedean standpoint" to explain how modern science has exchanged an earth-bound view of the human condition for a "truly universal viewpoint." In sections 36 through 40 of her book she discusses this Archimedean standpoint at some length, and these are among the most provocative sections of the book. Seventeenth-century science began to treat nature in mathematical terms and so demonstrated a large body of consequential truths that no longer relied on witnessing nature at "close range by human senses." Subsequent to this scientific revolution, the rise of Cartesian skepticism moved this Archimedean standpoint to the introspective realm of the individual subject and thus negated the truly shared and communal form of common sense. Many other thinkers and writers, from Comte to Eliot and Foucault, have offered versions of these revolutions in human thought, and it is less Arendt's uniqueness in this area that I mean to invoke than her reliance on such a historical scheme to explain her views of the modern world's political values. Snyder's views of this period's revolutions in mental habits—call it post-Renaissance science—coincide to a great extent with Arendt's, though he extends the period of "corruption" further back and locates his most obvious proof of its negative consequences in the misuse of natural resources. His attitude toward the "inner space" opened up by Cartesian introspection is also somewhat at variance with Arendt's, since for him the "power-vision in solitude" offers an important preserve of value and truth that must be safeguarded against all political intrusion.

Arendt's main point is that the modern world is most hampered by its elevation of action over contemplation, with the concomitant devaluation of thought itself within the realm of action. To restore to political vision the awareness of the value and necessity of thought, not only as a form of activity but also as its most fully human form: this is Arendt's central project, and it is close to Snyder's as well. From the objectivist poetics of *Riprap* and *Myths & Texts,* on to the personal doubt of *The Back Country,* and then through to the new senses of community and self-hood in *Earth House Hold* and *Turtle Island,* the curve of Snyder's career has been from the factlike density of perceptual intensity to the harmonious patternmaking of the immanently mythic imagination. Such a course of development has taken Snyder deeper and deeper into the workings of the political imagination as well.

At the same time, Snyder's artistic development has been equally deepened and yet balanced. I think that at his best Snyder is a moral visionary who is neither a scourge nor a satirist; that he has spoken as a prophet whose "tribe" is without definite national or cultural boundaries; and that he is a writer with deep allegiances to modernism who yet is not overridingly obsessed with verbal perfectionism for its own sake. In each of these balanced stances can be located his weaknesses as well as his strengths. Another way of stating this paradox at the heart of Snyder's work is to say that he wants more than most to overcome the alienation and isolation of the poet in the modern world, but the terms of his vision have, by their very extravagance, made him often seem a party of one. In this sense Snyder is a quintessential American artist, torn by an idealizing vision between opposing hungers for both a new sense of community and a new sense of radical individuality.

But rather than concentrate too much at the close on the tensions and contradictions in Snyder's work, I would like to end by stressing that he is above all a poet of celebration and ecstasy. As such, his vision must terminate with, or open out into, a utopian vista where the rightness of the political realm finally produces a world of plenitude. For me the best statement of Snyder's celebratory completion comes in one of the interviews in *The Real Work,* where he formulates an Archimedean point of his own. He has been talking about the limits of his own system of things, and how his stress on local awareness and regional consciousness may limit one's ability to respond to people who live in other places and with other cultural ties. Snyder's solution is to imagine the universal dimension of all human experience that is fully informed about its relation to both the earth and the world, a fullness "where all natures intersect." The healing he speaks of is the healing of the breach that physical and cultural separation might cause. What follows is a marvelous metaphoric interweaving of both human and natural fullness:

> This level of healing is a kind of poetic work that is forever "just begun." When we bring together our awareness of the worldwide network of folktale and myth imagery that has been the "classical tradition"—the lore-bearer—of everyone for ten thousand and more years, and the new (but always there) knowledge of the worldwide interdependence of natural systems, we have the biopoetic beginning of a new level of world poetry and myth. That's the beginning for this age, the age of knowing the planet as one ecosystem, our own little watershed, a community of people and beings, a place to sing and meditate, a place to pick berries, a place to be picked in.
>
> The communities of creatures in forests, ponds, oceans, or grasslands seem to tend toward a condition called climax, "virgin forest"—many species, old bones, lots of rotten leaves, complex energy pathways, woodpeckers living in snags, and conies harvesting tiny piles of grass. This condition has considerable stability and holds much energy in its web—energy that in simpler systems (a field of weeds just after a bulldozer) is lost back into the sky or down the drain. All of evolution may have been as much shaped by this pull toward climax as it has by simple competition between individuals or species. If human beings have any place in this

scheme it might well have to do with their most striking characteristic—a large brain, and language. And a consciousness of a peculiarly self-conscious order. Our human awareness and eager poking, probing, and studying is our beginning contribution to planet-system energy-conserving; another level of climax!

One way to appreciate fully the deeply human richness of this vision of plenitude is to see it as a liminal utopia, poised between fullness and yet more growth. Another way to see it is as a modern apocalypse that features woodpeckers and berry-picking. Either way, assuming the real work always includes some formulation of an ideal world, I would offer this vision as sufficient proof that Snyder has built a place for the mind to stay and to imagine more far-reaching harmonies while preserving all the wealth of the past. This, of course, is the world of his books where he is willing and even eager to give us another world both more ideal and more real than our own. The rest of the work is ours.